MW01242743

A
BIRD FLIES
WITH A
LIL MAGIC

KWAMI J. GREEN

A
BIRD FLIES
WITH A
LIL MAGIC

KWAMI J. GREEN

Table of Contents

Chapter 1

Rain pounded on the bus windows. No surprise there for Mikell. On the first day, bussed to World Leadership Prep, miles away from his Dorchester home, and the skies opened up. He could choose to think of it as a cleansing, he supposed. A rain that would soak and wash away the life behind him and clear the way for what was ahead...whatever the hell that would be.

Normally he found rain relaxing. Probably because he learned long ago to associate it with peace. Not even the hood rats that ran with gangs around the streets of his home wanted to be out in the soaking rain. The more rainy days, the less chaos and violence outdoors. The rain kept people inside, sticking close to their own crews, with less interaction with rivals, hence less violent ends to their meetings. When it rained at night, Mikell slept well. Throw in some thunder, and that sleep was damn near divine.

The bus nailed a pothole full of water, jarring the bus with an angry bounce, causing Mike's head, leaning against the window to pop suddenly and come knocking back on the glass. But he couldn't bear to care much. His hood pulled over his skull cap, hanging just over his eyes, and the headphones on his ears drowned out the world. One jolt wasn't going to break him from it.

His eyes did briefly open to scope out his surroundings. Being a young black man on a bus nearing the upscale Downtown Boston didn't exactly draw positive attention his way. The old woman sitting across from him when he last had his eyes open was still staring at him, but catching his eyes open up, she nervously looked away.

The heavy-set man standing nearby cast a glance in his direction, then down to the floor. He looked as if the shaking of the bus was getting to him. He was pale as a ghost. Mikell subtly pulled his feet back under him. If this dude was going to be sick, Mikell wanted to minimize his chances of being in the way. He had seen motion-sick riders vomit on public transport before.

He closed his eyes again and sunk back into the bumping drill rap that was playing in his ears. Mikell hoped to break away from reality for just a few more minutes. This music puzzled him by his attraction to it. It represented little of how he functioned and how the mechanics of his mind worked, but it was reminiscent of home, maybe through some type of sick link. The combination of the beats with the piercing rhetoric, with the stories of acts no one outside that "life" could really grasp...he didn't condone, but it's what he grew up with. He had questioned why he gravitated to them but never came up with anything except that it felt like home. What's more, he was pretty good at rapping himself.

But that shit needed to stay hidden and stowed away. His Pops struggled too damn hard and stressed way too much about every aspect of his own and Mikell's life to find out that his son felt a kinship to drill rapping. It would crack him. His old man didn't deserve that. Mikell often got fed up with his father's optimistic attitude in the face of constant setbacks and blatant discrimination. Even when he could keep steady work for a bit, Travis Sharp would endure some shit no man deserved, yet he would put it in the rearview mirror, chalk it up to the "you make the life you want to have" attitude that he constantly preached to his son. Of course, he never forgot the reality of the world in which they lived.

In Mikell's eyes, this outward optimism in the face of oppression was seriously questionable. His mind was set on viewing disrespect as a crime far greater than any actual crime in the eyes of the law. The gangs in the streets would not be disrespected. If you did, it would be at your own peril. Pops didn't get it. He swallowed the bull shit that his life and the people in it seemed to constantly hand him, and rolled along like it was just a bump in the road. In the meantime, the rolling wheels of the discrimination machine rolled straight over him.

It was out of respect to his pops that Mikell took this chance to be transferred out of his school with all the people he knew and the routine he was used to, to take his World Leadership Prep opportunity. Travis did everything to provide his son with a good life despite constantly being dealt a shit hand. Now, this opportunity straight up fell in his lap, like some kind of cosmic accident, and Mikell wanted none of it, but this is what Travis strived for, lived for, broke himself for. Turning this down would have crushed him. Mikell couldn't allow that. Pops was all he truly had for family.

Maybe Travis was a naively optimistic man, but his heart was all about Mikell. He kept Mikell out of the gang life, he forced him into studies when his friends were balling at the courts. At the time Mike was angry and felt rebellious even. But rarely did he disobey or act on his annoyance. It was just him and Pops, without that, he was just another broke-ass kid ripe for gang life. His old man saved his life over and over again without stepping in front of a bullet for him. It's a debt he could never repay, nor did he want to...but felt he had to.

The bus pulled to a hard stop. Mikell lazily opened his eyes and peeked out from under his hood. The old woman from across him was up and wearing his plastic parka cap was descending the bus stairs. He glanced up to check the bus stop. He studied the map to a photographic memory level. Two stops left. Just another 6 or 7 minutes and his life would flip upside down. Too late to go back?

He shut his eyes again, retracting his head back into his hood, and gave himself 4 minutes to drift off into the drill rap playing in his ears. Retracted is how he would be today, and moving forward. He was probably going to hate everything that came from today forward. The sideways glances at the kid from the hood who didn't belong, the utter sense of the unknown ahead, the questions from his boys about where fuck it is he was. Keeping the transfer on the DL seemed like a good idea at the time...

When his eyes opened he was mere blocks away. The rain poured as hard as before, with no sunshine in sight. The neighborhood around him was visibly different than where he got on the bus. Mikell shifted in his seat and pulled the hood down over his face. All he wanted to see was the floor and the ground. The beats filling his head will be his hook back to the life he knew, a soundtrack of home on the march into the unknown. He threw his backpack across his back and got up, slowly heading for the door. The heavy-set man was quick to take his seat.

The bus pulled up to the stop and screeched to a stop. Mikell pulled up on his belt, pulled the hood down in front of his eyes, and stepped off the bus into the abysmal rain.

Chapter 2

Mike stood in the doorway of the living room. Of all of the mornings for this to happen, this was the worst. His backpack slung over his right shoulder, Mike stared dumbly at his father standing over a passed-out Eric, slapping his face and screaming at him to wake up since he was freaking his mother out. Mike's mom sat on her knees near the couch that Eric was on, sobbing uncontrollably.

Mike knew he had only been standing at the bottom of the stairs for a few seconds, but it felt like a lifetime. He was terrified, but not at all surprised. Eric has long made this type of horrifying scenario possible. A knock at the door broke him from his shock trance. He quickly moved to it and turned the doorknob, allowing the two soaked EMTs to rush in the door. He silently lifted his finger to the living room doorway and they bolted in that direction, dragging the rain running from their persons all over the foyer and living room rugs. They knelt next to Eric to begin their examination. Mike stepped into the living room.

"Dad, what should....can...I do to..." - Mike stumbled out.

His father's head snapped around. "No....not now....go, Mike. This is going to be taken care of."

Mike stared dumbly. "Dad, I...." - he managed to utter.

"Go to school, damn it!" - snapped Bill. "You got tryouts, tests, and way too little time to get to school. Don't you dare throw that into chaos and ruin your future like...." - he paused, wiping the sweat from his forehead. Bill Cassidy was always prone to start pouring sweat when he was stressed and scared, regardless of the temperature in the room. Finding his older son unresponsive on the couch first thing in the morning and not being able to do anything to calm his inconsolable wife was more than a trigger for it. "...just go, Mike! Things will be fine. Let them do what they need to do."

Mike was at a loss. How in the world would this be fine? He looked over at his crying mother and stepped forward to try to comfort her. "Mike, get your ass out that door right now! Enough is going on. Keep some normality going today for fuck's sake!" - William snapped again. Mike retracted.

Hesitantly, he moved towards the door, his eyes still on Eric. Stepping outside, it was the first drops of water from the damn waterfall from the sky that broke his trance. He reached backward to snag his hood, which had been trapped under his backpack, and wrestled it loose, pulling it over his head. He finally turned to the doorway. He realized he was holding his AirPods in his hand when he ran downstairs to see what his mother was screaming about. He finally turned away and threw them in his ears. Time to make a run for it.

***

Not a great day for concentration...not at all. He was ready for his chem test, or at least he thought he was. No word about his brother's condition, and it was past noon. Mike and Eric were not particularly close, but they weren't constantly at odds either. Eric was six years older and he had been babied quite a bit by the Cassidy parents. Yet there were always high expectations of him. Perhaps the sudden realization that he skated by with ease until shit got serious in life, and coasting would no longer do, is what sent Eric down his drug-fueled spiral.

As for most, it started off experimentally, but it was obvious to everyone around that this was no mere "phase" after a while. Like most addicts, the lure of drugs sucked Eric in more and more, and off he went, down the rabbit hole of harder and harder substance indulgence, always chasing a better high. Mike wasn't sure which of the many potential variants of slow killers Eric consumed last night or this morning, but this is not the first time he had given his family a fright.

Eric's decline and degeneration were quick and it was obvious, apparently to everyone except for their father, at least in an expression of concern. William Cassidy was a traditionalist in a sense. He was a caring and loving father, but he hid those things under the guise of authoritative decrees and rigorous discipline. He was hard on his sons, but if they ever needed help, he was there. In some ways, he set high expectations for everyone in his life, including himself, and would feel like a hypocrite if he did not follow through on them himself. If only they weren't so rooted in the past.

The drawback with William is that even though it was clear that Eric was descending into a drug-fueled junkie mode, William tried to mask the life in his home as a very standard, respectably successful family. After all, this was a private issue and it wasn't anybody's business, right?

William served as a foreman for a local (yet reputable) construction company, and he prided himself on holding an efficiency-freak attitude, veiled by business-faced clout. If you worked to your maximum potential, there would be no problems. If something prevented you from doing so, you were just dragging everyone else's potential down. If you weren't a well-oiled cog, operating smoothly and efficiently, available whenever to corporate machine was running, you needed to be replaced. It's a grim view of people, but as the operator of said machine, that's the standard William held. Apparently, his blind spot was for problems in his own home. Eric was the prime example there.

Their expectations of Mike were somewhat less when he was younger. So while William internally recognized Eric's "fall from grace", he withheld that recognition externally. The only hint of it Mike saw was that the expectations for him to perform and be a success exponentially increased as the prospects for his older brother and his "illness" were. Now, Mike was to be the successful heir to the Cassidy family.

Mike's mother never treated her sons differently, but she also withheld her opinions and concerns in terms of really vital matters about pretty much everything. Eric's condition was no exception. Mike supposed that this is why the ugly reality of that morning is what finally broke her. Ann was a great mom, and she didn't deserve the misery, but she was also not entirely realistic at times. In much in the same way that his father externally denied any familial issues, she chose rosy-side optimism, in nearly every situation. Mike found this charming when he was a young kid, now it was just annoying.

Mike wasn't the best student, but he was far from a failure too. He knew his problem was that his mind wandered far too much. Concentration was not his strong suit. But two things definitely held his focus: sports and music. He had been watching basketball with his brother and dad since before he could speak, and one of his best memories was going to a playoff Celtics game when he was eight. A kid from Boston being bound to basketball was almost a sure thing given the town's proud basketball heritage. He didn't recall too much from that age, but he could recite the events of that game blow by blow. Not surprisingly, he stuck with the basketball obsession and had been playing every single year. His father always spoke of Larry Bird, and from an impressionable young age, Mike regarded the Boston legend as a bit of a hero.

While he never lost his mind over Mike's basketball success, a blind man could see the elation in William Cassidy's eyes when he watched Mike play. He didn't make it to many games, prioritizing work over recreational school activities, but he made it a point to exude a lot more support for Mike once Eric's social and personal declines became evident. On some level, William knew that Mike was hovering on the average of academic success, but on the court, he could count on his son to be a triumph.

World Leadership Prep needed a star, and while a couple of shining lights cut through the otherwise murky team when Mike made the team, things took a turn. Mike was not the sole reason of course, but his contributions were apparent. No championships to speak of, but there was a lot more hope. Mike knew that basketball was his way to college if he remained healthy. Then he would focus on his academic performance.

While Mike sifted through a variety of music genres, rap resonated with him most. It started on a subconscious level he thought, the beats reminded him of a basketball bounce, linking his two favorite things in his mind. When he listened to rap or he was on the court, he was in the zone unlike in the classroom. His frustrations over his brother's obvious condition and his parents' seeming blind eye to it, riled up a load of frustration. He tried to be conscious about not letting it out, but it manifested through other mediums. Sometimes it was a torrent of aggressive play on the court, other times it was at the expense of his classmates.

When he was introduced to drill rap, it seemed like a natural fit. He had read before that listening to aggressive music when you are hurt, mad, or stressed, made you feel better. After testing this theory out, he had no doubt about the truth of that statement. Listening to drill rap also took his mind out of the problems in his life, the gated misery of his family situation, and the aggression he would otherwise take out on others in some way.

But there was no music now and no court to calm his nerves. There were just two vital tests, and he was trying to get his wits about him for just the first one. The pressure of all of this, not letting things slip so he can still have his basketball, compounded by the not-knowing and the concern for his brother, left next to zero room for him to actually have a functioning mind.

Mike just wanted to be done with this day right now. But it was a long way from being done. Basketball tryouts were right after school. When the hell would he know about Eric? There was just too much going on.

***

"Fucked that up...hard!." - Mike said to Asher Flannigan, the basketball team's shooting guard and one of his only friends. Asher befriended Mike from early on in the school year and the two seemed to hit it off from day one, but Asher tended to have an attitude about him that was not what Mike considered likable. Nor did he have an uplifting disposition.

"The first test of the year, so you got time to make it right. Chill Cassidy. I'm gonna call you MCass, to boost your luck...." - Asher gave the cheesy joke a moment to breathe before continuing. "Like the test....anyways...ready to get your starting power forward position? Saw some new blood in line at signups. We can shit all over them on the court. A couple of newbies too. Looked like some ghetto rats got picked up from the pity-city bus. They show up here and their think their skin qualifies them to jump on the basketball court. Smoke those assholes tonight Mike! Humiliation will teach them."

"Aha...wait...what? Oh yeah...yeah, I heard they are doing some outreach thing. Not worried about it. I got enough shit on my mind to worry about that." - Mike responded, distracted.

"The fuck, bro?! Am I still talking to Mike Cassidy, the guy who talks about posterizing every fucking defender? Don't let whatever this shit is stop you from doing that to these hoodie charity cases." - Asher bit back.

Mike glared at him, trying to suppress his anger about that comment. Obviously, he didn't know what was going on. "This 'shit' is real-world shit, so get off my ass." He turned and headed the other way.

Asher shuffled around uncomfortably for a moment. "....whatever....real shit can step aside for balling..." - he muttered, his voice lowering from the start of the sentence to the end.

Chapter 3

The summers in Boston are hard to predict. Sometimes oppressive heat and sticky humidity cover the area, while other times there is a sharp drop in temperatures, resulting in randomly cool days and nights. Predicting Boston weather is a bit of a running joke in the area. People know it's erratic, yet constantly complain that the weather "professionals" on TV can't get their weather right. If you want to know the weather, look outside. If you don't like the weather, wait a few minutes. One place where the heat was not unpredictable though, was on the courts of the BNBL.

If one was to seek out a prideful bunch of tough scrappers, Boston would be a great place to start. The city's rich sports history spans every major sport as the Patriots, Bruins, and Red Sox have had their chance to shine on the top of their respective mountains. Historically though, Boston's heart lies in its basketball roots. From the Bird and Parish era to the triple threat of Pierce, Garnett, and Allen, Boston's basketball sports a storied history. And while other sports have siphoned some of the limelight in more recent events, the love for the game of basketball has never abandoned the city.

In an attempt to keep the basketball-loving community fed with their insatiable hunger for sports and to promote a sense of socially healthy competition, the city of Boston set up the Boston Neighborhood Basketball League (BNBL) with the idea of having the most talented youth of the city come out to represent their neighborhoods. Boston itself is not a large place, but the greater metro-Boston area that expands from as far north as Charlestown to as far south as Hyde Park and as far west as Brighton offers a healthy mix of neighborhoods full of competitive spirits hungry to represent their share of the city.

The competition is played all over Boston, but the finals land the winning teams on a court outside of Fenway Park, where the summer heat really gets cranked as locals from the represented neighborhoods, as well as others, show up to watch the best of the best settle which neighborhood is the top dog in Boston's basketball realm.

Bostonians are a proud bunch, so to them, the BNBL finals might as well be the world championship. Community from the areas select their few best players and those match up against each other, with a pair of coaches selecting the cream-of-the-crop. The young men who show up to ball are starving lions on the courts, armed with an unquenchable thirst for victory, pride, and respect, with a sprinkle of hope of being noticed by basketball recruiters. The BNBL was also the first place to bring together the representatives from Dorchester and Southie just two summers ago.

Dorchester is a largely minority-populated part of the greater Boston area, though occasionally sprinkled with classier neighborhoods, has long been considered one of South Dorchester's more turbulent areas. Populated largely by minorities who, through little fault of their own, have been pushed to live, or rather survive, in subpar financial conditions.

Southie (a local moniker for South Boston) has been occupied largely by the descendants of Irish immigrants, who, in their own way have felt oppressed. Reflective of their own hardships they have watched as their government in an attempt to help keep citizens financially afloat, trafficked living finances to Boston's poorest, while they worked hard in crappy jobs that barely made a dent in their living expenses, and felt like they received no help. It is no wonder that their frustration and ire frequently turned on the minorities. Dorchester, falling into a category of such a case with many of its residents, therefore was one of the places the Irish folk in Southie looked to with anger, staring through a prism of injustice. Dorchester residents just viewed Southie as bitter, entitled, and racist white clowns who blamed other races for their own shortcomings.

With the already brewing background of these two locations being palpable, for their basketball teams to meet in the BNBL finals sure felt like a punchline to a joke of cosmic proportions. The road was certainly not paved for their arrival at the finals. They weren't the best teams, but they had drive and talent. A team of black young men possessed the cleverness and ankle-snapping speed that led them to the rim with epic levels of drive. The largely white Southie boys had their own speed demons on the squad, plus a pair of lights-out shooters whose uncanny three-point consistency was jarring. They lived by the three far more than died by one.

And yet, neither neighborhood was thought to have a chance. Their teams played with bare necessities, while Roxbury and Charlestown teams recruited professionals to assist the coaches. It was poetic in a way that they pulled out some squeakers to arrive in the finals to face each other.

The BNBL finals that year brought Dorchester and Southie into the rectangle arena. Battling one another for court supremacy and the title of Boston's biggest baller court badasses. The Dorchester team featured a quiet but hyper-focused Mikell Sharp. Southie had a promising power forward named Mike Cassidy.

***

The neighborhoods drew some seriously intense representation. The police questioned the wisdom of the Boston mayor permitting this event to take place outside of Fenway, a tourist-heavy area by day, and a bar-hopping scene by night. While normally the police would prefer to keep the press at arm's length, they began to believe that adding a level of a spectacle to the BNBL finals could keep the rowdy crowds from being too intense. They didn't even mind their own cameo appearances on the footage being recorded for local coverage.

Unfortunately, these types of events don't just bring the prideful fans around but draw in many seedy characters who want to make a buck or two....or a thousand, off their desired bets. It has been the worst kept secret in Boston that players in the BNBL finals have been accosted by gang members from other neighborhoods with demands that they derail their team's efforts if they knew what was good for them. On the other hand, their own side demanded that they either win at all costs or lose without making it seem intentional. It has never been proved, but strong suspicions of such pressures affecting finals in the past were not uncommon.

Neither Mike nor Mikell was safe from these looming intimidations either. Not long before the game, a slew of gang members approached Mike Cassidy and some teammates as they were heading to the courts early for some shoot around warm-ups and told them Dorchester was going to kick their asses, and if the results of the game were anything aside from a total domination blowout, they would need to watch their asses in the streets. Southie kids were not pushovers and they addressed this by obnoxious smirks and waving off the threatening menaces. Probably not the wisest thing, but they figured these guys would be rolling back to Dorchester regardless of the result, and their team did not work their asses off to lay down in the finals because of some hoodlum threats.

There was also, of course, the mob. They were a bit more subtle, offering up some compliments and telling the Southie team how much of a shame it would be if they lost, as well as if they didn't send the Dorchester "coloreds" home with not just an L in the BNBL, but with a few missing teeth or torn ligaments. The veiled threats from the mob were more intimidating, but ultimately, they did not want to put themselves in the public eye or in the crosshairs of the cops (more than they already had been), so they would likely stay subtle with their actions, especially those dealing with the BNBL game...unless they had made some heavy bets on the match up. Mike Cassidy liked to tell himself that he was just not that important.

Mikell Sharp encountered pressure from Dorchester gang members long before he arrived to play the Southie kids. Put up to their initiation trials, the gang-sent newbies with a message that was delivered not-at-all discretely had Mikell trying not to sweat it, but the lingering nerves, not for himself, but for Pops, were always there.

At the end of the day, most of these ended up being idle threats that fizzled out. Besides, there was too much pride on the line for their neighborhoods to simply throw in the towel for some threats. After all, they had the backing of most of their region behind them. Making it to the finals of the BNBL put enough attention on the players that anyone thinking of harming them would attract many of the eyes of the law in their direction. Gangs knew better than to go looking for this kind of attention, and organized crime syndicates certainly wanted to steer clear.

So the BNBL stayed on course with players coming in with blazing dunks, fire-off three-pointers, and moves that made the crowds go nuts. The BNBL did what most Boston sports tend to do, build more rivalries than it did bridges, despite idealistic hopes.

Mikell and Mike would meet each other in the BNBL finals. It's a safe bet that neither one thought that their paths would ever cross again....

Chapter 4

The BNBL finals were going to be big. Mikell and Mike were quite aware of that. The nerves, excitement, stress, and pride of the event, compounded by the weight of representing their respective neighborhoods, were all either could carry. Coming back on the losing end was not an option for either one of the boys, for their own reasons.

Mike Cassidy, known since a younger age to his friends as "Bird" (aptly after his adopted childhood hero) for his seemingly uncanny shooting prowess, certainly felt the rush of the day, but he would have given anything to have been elsewhere when the BNBL ended on the day of the finals. It was bad enough that he was in the eye of that hurricane. What made it worse is the haunting that this would cast on his dreams, or more accurately, his nightmares from that day forward.

The elation he felt as the shots dropped for him was unparallel. He surprised himself. A power forward nailing three after three, following up with a crossover layup, and a stunning, posterizing dunk on Dorchester's center was not something Mike would have ever forecasted for his game performance. Had the BNBL finals gone off in a path of classic competition, he would have reveled in those memories. But the actual conclusion to his day was far from anything relating to pride.

Dorchester was certainly no pushover, the game was tight, never having more than seven points separating the two teams on the board, but as the game went on, the beauty of the game was overtaken by geographical pride chest-beating. Like warring nations on a battlefield of the court, the somewhat honorable warriors armed with the round fox-orange sphere of rubber and hide as their weapon of choice, the battle of the BNBL finals was turning out truly epic. But much like highly invested clans overlooking the scene of warriors sworn to a fair contest, the crowds of the proud Boston bunch were not going to be happy with an ending to such a spar...no matter what that ending was.

***

Mikell Sharp, known to his friends as "Magic" thanks to his speed skills in cutting through opposing defenses on the court, walked off the court, sweat drowning his eyes, fury pounding in his heart. Ejected for his fifth foul, in a game of his lifetime. The impressively accurate white boy on the Southie team who has been torching them with threes, as his team staved off a crushing lead by their sheer dominance on the boards, was on the stripe. And for what? For a foul that never happened.

"Fucking Southie mob bastards made it to the zebras...no fucking way that was a foul. Take the opportunity to eject me from the game when I'm burning hot. This is some bull shit!" - fumed Mikell as he stormed off the court after getting the face of a pugnacious and unrepentant ref. "Who hired these guys to ref this game anyway?"

He wiped the sweat out of his eyes and flicked his arm to the side sending droplets flying off to the side. From the corner of his eye, he saw the coach. The man was intense-looking as it is, this was the most fumed Mikell had ever seen him. The veins were popping out of his neck. This game hung on by a point, and now the Southie team's best player was at the stripe, and the clock had less than forty seconds to tick away. This was fucked up, in the worst way possible. Dorchester would not take this shit.

The crowd was already worked up to a fever pitch, but that last foul was too much. Something was going to happen, Mikell knew it from the start, he was just hoping it would not be anything the cops couldn't quell within a minute or two. He could hear the Dorchester contingent slinging profanities and slamming up against the fences gating the court, while the Southie crew piled on the racial slurs along with taunts.

Mikell kicked a water bottle that exploded just off the court. He would not look at anyone. How could he face them now? The moment owned him right now. He snatched the nearest towel, not giving a shit that it was covered in someone else's sweat, and slammed his body down on the bench, draping the towel over his head.

The whistle blew, but that is the only sound Mikell could hear above the fervor of the crowd and his own pulse pounding inside of his head. The game stood at a one-point difference, Dorchester hanging on to the lead for dear life. Now two foul shots could turn the tide. He knew he should be a team player but he could not bring himself to watch this happen now. There was no fucking foul!

**

The atrocity broke the crowd's pressure cooker of a temper. No one seemed sure of where the bottle came from. The shattering of the glass startled Mike Cassidy, bringing him out of his concentration daze. He couldn't think straight anyway, the basket seemed like a pinhole, positioned far away. He would need to be a straight-up sniper to hit this one. Let alone for two shots. Then the fragile peace around the court was smashed with the sound of shattered glass. How fucking poetic!

Mike whipped his head around, terrified of what he saw. He felt alone, like a man stuck in a cage with starving, untamed lions crawling outside of the cage that housed his arena. There was nowhere to go. Steve

Olson, the Southie center, a big bulky mass of a human stepped behind Mike and edged him toward the exit.

"Go before the shit really goes off, Cassidy!" - Olson shouted in his ear.

Mike was not going to chance to have the finals mark his final day on the planet so he moved toward the gate. Two Dorchester kids ripped through heading right toward him. Olson went to step in front but three Irish thugs cut them off, tackling one to the ground.

Suddenly, what seemed like a torrent of police uniforms ripped through the now open gate. This slowed down the flow of the rioters. The police quickly positioned themselves with their backs to the Southie players, who were now quickly herded into a corner of the court and moved seamlessly toward the door, gradually forcing the Southie team in that direction as well. It occurred to Mike that this move was very much by design. As he tried to peek around the chaos, he found himself transfixed on the Dorchester team who was being surrounded by Boston PD much in the same way that the Southie team was. He could see the kid whose foul call sparked this insanity. He was at the edge of a police circle being gradually backed out of the court as well. Ruthless Southie mobsters were pushing their way right toward the circle of cops, determined to get at the Dorchester team. Mike didn't know whether to feel pride in his Southie supporters or shame for their reckless, insane behavior.

Looking around, Mike Cassidy stopped moving toward the gate. Then he was forced by the jarring push from a powerful hand of the Southie center. Olson shoved Mike out of the open gate, a giant hand on his shoulder, and pressed him along down the street. Mike was worried for those left behind, but right now, he needed to be away, his team knew it, and he was not going to play the hero. Did enough of that out on the court, and look what happened.

***

Sidestepping the rushing cops, Mikell Sharp bolted for the door. The hulking figure of the Southie center was pressing another Southie player out of the gate, with two other teammates and the coach following shortly after. He saw his teammates backing up in the corner. One was swinging fists at the approaching men. Suddenly the influx of police jerseys surrounded them, keeping the oncoming onslaught of the rioters away. He was suddenly squeezed in a semi-circle of black and blue, and the officers shifted left and backward. He realized they were gathering the Dorchester players and moving them closer to the court gate.

A woman on the sidelines screamed like a damn banshee. He turned to look, only to be shoulder checked by a big frame of a bald, black police officer backing up towards him. The officer glanced back angrily, giving Mikell the hint to keep his ass moving. Mikell felt the urge to stay and intervene. He couldn't help but feel like his melodramatic walk-off after the bullshit call really broke the uneasy peace of the crowd riled up by the competitive fury. But he had to find Pops, he was around here. Mikell needed to keep him safe.

With eyes locked on the ground, Mikell headed for the nearest door, shoving his way through a pouring tidal wave of Dorchester and Southie fans pouring into the chaos. He had a feeling someone was going to stop him and he would be involved anyway. If he did, the wrath would be one he brought on himself with his behavior, and he knew it. He had been around gangs, but they traveled in smaller numbers committing their shit in the streets. This was escalating into a full-on riot. When it's time to go, it's time to really go.

There would be fallout, and he would deal with it when it came. Now, he had to find Pops, and get both of their asses as far away from his before the cops siphoned him into the crowd of guilty rioters. And to hell with the game...

***

Mike Cassidy knew the call that set off the riot was a garbage one, but it was a tight game, and it was the ref who called it. He didn't know what was behind it, but the idea of a tainted ref in a game that good where he shined as bright as he did pissed him off. And the kid it was called against, great to have him a non-factor in the game because he would be the end of Southie's chances had he been allowed to stay in. Mike supposed in another, riot-free scenario he should have been thankful, but he felt filthy for even thinking it.

The eerie silence of the bus ride was interrupted only by honking and the angry grumbles from the bus driver, as he navigated his way through the impossible Southie streets. Mike's forehead was pressed against the bus window as he found himself zoned out, deep in thought. Basketball was a passion for him, but he loved the competition and the competitive spirit. He never got the religious ferocity of Boston fans towards their sports. If they weren't winning, did these rioters think they would force the ref to call the game for Southie or for Dorchester?

Mike wanted to give them more credit than that, but deep inside he knew...he had seen it in the eyes and heard it in the voices of his Irish neighbors and classmates. There was such resentment and so much vile. Probably why his decision to keep his admiration for rap was something he largely kept to himself.

Forced onto the team bus, damn near two at a time into doors, forced Mikell to scramble for the first seat he could find. He slid his sweaty torso toward the window and stared out at the end of the block where the police were holding the rioters back. One guy broke free and ran toward the bus. The doors closed before he was halfway there. The coach yelled to the bus driver to leave as the gears switched. The bus edged out into the street. Mikell watched the winded rioter run out of breath and be chased down by a cop. They were clear of the madness. Mikell Sharp suspected, however, that this was not a day they would purge from the team's memories.

The call was bad, the kid at the line would have sunk the free throws and put Southie up. Mikell was intrigued at what would have happened next. The emotion of the moment really got to him out there, and stomping off after insulting the ref...well it was cathartic, but it wasn't worth all this shit that followed..

Chapter 5

The BNBL finals never had a final whistle, the scoreboard could have read anything at the end, and the world would simply never know what would have been. That didn't stop people from playing up their side as the victor of course. The people of Dorchester and Southie both took the win to be their own. One team led when the game stopped, so they must have one. The other team would have gotten the ball for the majority of the remaining time with at most a point lead, so all the changes in the world were there for a victory. It was all maybes, but to the proud citizens of the districts of the BNBL finals, their team had won.

Beneath their claims to their team's victory, lay the sour underpinnings of who was at fault for the way the BNBL finals actually completed. The game wasn't finished, yet victory was claimed by both sides. But the unfinished business was clearly the fault of the other side. People are funny that way. Their hypocrisy is self-justified if it placates their own bias.

The fact of the matter was that no one actually knew who would have won, much like no one knew who threw the bottle that might as well have been a molotov cocktail tossed on a pilot light just waiting to burst into a raging inferno. The events of the BNBL finals were disastrous, and the events leading to them, well, those were as clear as mud.

The even more unfortunate effect is that the rivalry, animosity, and hostility between Southie and Dorchester only intensified. It was always there, but what could have been contained to the basketball courts spilled over onto the streets, into the schools, and the homes of the residents of those sections of Boston. The city's opposites were now more fringe than ever in their view of each other.

Mikell Sharp and Mike Cassidy faced more talk about the BNBL finals and their roles in the endless conclusion of the game than either of them could stomach. As the central figures of that controversy, ironically neither one saw the insistence of their fanbase as truth. Both knew the game of a lifetime for each of them would forever be damned to the controversy that stung its existence. There have been many BNBL finals, there will be many more, and theirs was the one with a fat asterisk slapped on it.

The people of Dorchester and the citizens of Southie could polish that turd all they wanted, but the sad truth is that it was still swimming in the bowl of Kool-Aid that they had collectively seemed to be drinking from. With time, all that anyone will remember will be the BS, with the actual events of the BNBL being lost in the chaotic confusion of people's single-stranded memories.

***

"Mike...Mike...Cassidy...kid!"

Mike Cassidy faintly heard the call through the drill rap he had zoned out to emanating from his headphones as he was leaving school. He began to turn as a stong, callous hand patted his shoulder. Mike turned with a start and pulled the headphones from his ears.

"How loud are you cranking those beats there kid? I could hear it from your headpiece standing half a dozen feet from ya!" - said the man standing near face to face with Mike at this point.

"Anyways, listen..." - the man said as he began padding his jacket and reached into the pocket of his worn yet incredibly comfortable-looking long sleeve jacket. Mike instinctively stepped back. The man was in his late 40s or early 50s and had skin that looked dark in a bit of an unnatural way, like someone who tanned successfully but a bit too much. He smelled like he overdid deodorant application to cover up the scent of sweat, but not with great success. Mike's brain associated the smell with post-game locker rooms.

"Whoa...hold up, what is happening right now?" - Mike spit out as the man began to pull an envelope from his jacket pocket. Mike hesitated. He was about to speak but decided to let this play out. If this guy was going to annoy him, he was just going to take off and bolt around the corner, jump into a store, or a potential doorway. He wasn't in the headspace to knock out some crazy old-timer.

The man finally produced the envelope in its full form, took a glance at it, like he was checking something out, then extended his arm to Mike. Mike looked at the envelope, then up at the guy's face. There was a brief glimpse of a smile that quickly removed itself from his face as he realized that Mike was not extending his hand back to pick the envelope up. After taking a moment, Mike slowly went for the envelope.

"What is this..?" - he asked, intentionally adding an infliction of bothered annoyance masking his curiosity in his tone.

"Your future, I hope. Take it home, give it a read. My contact information is in there. I encourage you to seriously consider this opportunity. Your showing at BNBL was impressive. You got a talent to harness there, son. Good fortune smiles on you, obviously, great performance, going to the line on an obviously wrong call to seal the game...if the unfortunate riot didn't prevent it. Could have been your day of victory, but your audience...well...seems like they were there more for just on-court competition, they came for a fight, they just needed an excuse. But you, you don't need to be known as the kid at the line when the BNBL riot broke out. You have potential, you have the drive, and you have...it, as they say. I know it, and I suspect you know it too. In that envelope is a chance to let everyone else know it too, without the riots getting in your way."

Mike realized his jaw was hanging open a bit so he pulled it shut. This was...unexpected. Obviously, the BNBL finals weren't overshadowed by the insanity at the end. Perhaps his performance really did get noticed. Mike took the envelope and started to open it.

"I suggest you wait till you are in a good headspace and in a quiet place to sit down and read that. I wouldn't want you to make rash decisions or come to hasty judgments. Take it in, understand it, and talk to your family. Not going to happen without their green light anyhow, but I encourage you to advocate strongly for this with them if you want it. These opportunities...let's just say, are fleeting, and many of us would have loved to grab onto a rope when freefalling into the abyss, but only some of us did." - the man interjected.

Mike paused. "I'm not falling into anything and not looking for a rope, but fine. I'll read it later. If I'm interested, I guess we'll speak again."

A brief smile snuck to the man's face before hiding itself in the resolve of his glare. "You're right and I look forward to it." He extended his hand to Mike. "Randall Lancing."

Mike, shook his hand unenthusiastically. "Mike Cassidy."

"Safe bet I knew who I was talking to, kid. I'll look forward to talking to you soon. You make the decision best for you, but opportunities like this don't come for everyone. Don't miss out if you don't have to." He patted Mike on the side of his shoulder, turned around, and headed down the street, leaving Mike with the envelope in his hand.

***

Mikell Sharp was lost in his favorite drill rap beats as he instinctively prepared to jot up the stairs to his father's Dorchester apartment. He stopped short as he almost ran over a guy sitting on the stairs. Mike glanced up, at the guy speaking to him, and realized all he could hear in his ears was the drill rap. He pulled down his headphones.

"....attention than on the court...oh, got it, zoned out ha? I appreciate escaping the real world for the musical one as much as the next guy. Seems to be a common thing with the generation. I presume you are Mikell?" - Mikell finally got to hear from the man on his steps.

"Who's asking?" - Mikell snapped back more harshly than he intended. This must be a reporter or a local blogger. They've tried to contact him since the BNBL, and he was in no mood.

"Randall Lancing, or Coach Lancing for my guys. So you are Mikell then...Mikell Sharp. The infamous BNBL victim of the shit call that sparked the match next to the powderkeg?" - Lancing replied.

Mikell stayed quiet. The man had a point, but damn, he was blunt with it.

"Too far? Too soon? I guess this is not a great approach to what I'm here for. Apologies, my smart mouth has gotten me into some heat before. Listen..." - Lancing stood up. Mikell noticed he had what looked like a manilla envelope by his side. "You got talent on the court Sharp, and you would be wasting it if you didn't leverage it effectively. I want to offer you a chance to do so. Before you say no and dismiss me as some hack, I'm going to ask you to take this with you and give it a read, and attentive one. Talk it over with your folks, the decision will probably be a tough one, but, for many reasons, a worthwhile one too."

Lancing extended an envelope to Mikell. Mikell didn't move. "What is this? I ain't taking mystery handouts. I don't want your money to blog your hit pieces on."

"Ah...I see the journalist vultures have already come for your soul. Well, luckily that's not what I'm here for. This is an opportunity for your benefit and mine...in a sense. But my benefit is that I get to coach the future of basketball, to you, this is an open door to elevating yourself and your folks from one place to a whole other level. Plus, it would be pretty weird for a blogger or a journalist to call themselves "coach" no?" - He extended the envelope again.

After about 4 seconds which felt like 10 minutes, Mikell finally took the envelope from his hand.

"My contact info is included for when you are ready. I normally say no pressure but, the time is a bit of the essence, so I really advise you not to drag your feet on this one. This one is a ....sure thing, as they say, if you're willing to work for it." - Lancing patted Mikell on the shoulder and headed down the stairs, leaving Mikell in a bit of a daze with the envelope in his hand. Mikell glanced back at the man heading down the street. This guy must have been selling something. Talking it up like a life-changing turnaround like that? Who would buy this shit?

Mikell headed up into his apartment. Pops wasn't around, so all he could hear was his neighbor's TV, on way too loud as usual. Mikell tossed the envelope on the kitchen table and threw his headphones back on.

Chapter 6

Mikell Sharp slept in on Saturday mornings usually, but that Saturday he was stirred from his sleep. There was a nagging feeling weighing on him. He knew what it was all too well. The envelope handed to him by Coach Lancing contained an intriguing letter. It got a quiet read and then placed right back in the envelope. There was undeniable intrigue in joining a team as a walk-on star, and helping turn another team around, but he had his life in Dorchester. For better or worse, at least this life was undeniably his own. The type of change this called for was clearly a bridge too far.

Mikell shut his eyes, but sleep was not coming back. He hadn't checked the time, but his internal clock felt that it was absurdly early on a Saturday to be awake. He didn't meet to ball on the courts with his friends until 11, and he had nothing by time until then. He finally stretched and swung his feet off his bed. He craned his neck to the left, then to the right in a morning routine that had become habitual, hearing some concerningly loud, yet satisfying crackles and pops. Shaking off the dizzy-headedness that hit him after, Mikell dropped down to the ground and started on his daily push-up counts. Another morning ritual born of habit retained out of desire.

He followed the push-ups with the rest of his 5-minute workout routine, then grabbed the t-shift he threw across the back of his chair last night, gave it the smell test, deciding it wasn't awful, so he pulled it back on. Rubbing his eyes and his face, Mikell wandered out of his room and into the kitchen. He could smell Pops's coffee, and he would usually partake, but this morning he was awake enough. He padded through the kitchen, crossing into the living room and heading in the direction of the bathroom.

After the sweet relief on the porcelain throne, he washed his hands and headed back out. He shut off the bathroom light and looked into the living room to find Travis Sharp sitting back on his lazy boy chair, Travis's favorite living room accessory.

"Good sleep? - he asked with a slight smile.

"I've had better" - replied Mikell, suddenly noticing what Travis was holding in his hand. It was a stack of papers, immediately recognizable by the manilla envelope in Travis's lap.

"Too bad. Sit down with me a minute." - Travis said, leaning back into his chair.

"Pops I uh....gotta...." Mikell began to mutter.

"Won't take long. Sit, son." - Travis insisted.

Mikell drew in a breath. He wished that he had been more discreet with the paperwork. Part of him wished he didn't let his indecisiveness keep the thing around. He wished he just tossed it in the trash when he had a chance. He figured this conversation would happen eventually, but he was irked by the fact that it was about to happen now. He was not sure his thoughts were organized enough to do so, nor did he particularly want to start his weekend off in this manner. But with all that, he was not going to disrespect his old man. Mikell sat on the couch.

"Thanks, son. Now, I'd ask if you forgot to tell me about anything, but I think this might have been neglected for a reason. You know I ain't the kind to snoop on your business, but a blank manilla on the kitchen table with no labels except for your name, a man has to check it out. Didn't realize that inside I would find a key for my boy to his future." - Travis mused.

"Pops, I.....can we talk about this later." - Mikell was getting desperate to get out of this conversation. But he knew Pops, and he would have a better chance of seeing an eclipse today.

"Later, when time runs out? Later, when your chance at an escape from our gritty reality is gone? Later, when your life's best chance at moving up in the world passes you by?"

"Pops, now you're just being dramatic. I am not ignoring it, just thinking about it, ok?" - Mikell came off more defensive than he intended to.

"World Leadership Prep invites you to be on their basketball squad, a team that needs a turnaround, and an education that would cost a rich man a small fortune to afford, handed to you for free, full ride, and you are thinking about it? Listen, son, I want you to think about every action you take and all the big decisions you make, but some don't take long to consider. This is a chance you won't get again, and what kind of father would I be if I let you just blow this off?" - Travis sat up with a serious look on his face.

"Come on Pops" - Mikell felt a bit heated but was not ready to take it out on his old man. "Think about this for a minute. What chance is there that this is even legit? I don't know this Lancing guy from a hole in the ground. My team is here in Dorchester, my brothers are here, my life is here....shit, we can't afford the damn bus commute anyway!"

"Well hell son, I didn't think about that bus commute. Sounds like a real deal-breaker for a shot at tons of open doors in the future. I guess we'll scrap this opportunity over a bus fare." - Travis stared at Mikell for a response, deadpan. This positive, jovial man was not fucking around, just smacking his hesitant son around with some dark sarcasm.

42

"Real funny Pops. Like I said, my life is here. We get by, we make due, we get by like we always had. How do you think I'm going to fit into this white boy school. You want me to be the token black kid who comes out and puts up some points against their basketball opponents. Want me to be looked at as "he's alright, cuz he's our black" kid? Do you want your son to be the poster boy for posterizing white boys? What benefit is there to this? They need a better basketball team, so they come to mooch off the black kid who got heated and set off a riot...." - that was the first time Mikell ever verbally acknowledge to anyone that he felt at least somewhat responsible for the BNBL finals' insanity. He caught himself, took a breath, and was about the speak again when Travis raised his hand.

"Perspective, son. That's what life is all about. You can look at any situation from a negative viewpoint. There are a hundred reasons you can come up with why you should squander this opportunity, 3 or 4 might actually be pretty logical. But after that, your reasons just become excuses. But there are many more to go for it. I raised my son to read situations around him well. It's why you are so damn good on the courts. The mental game is the only way your physical court skills work, so use your capable brain to think this one through. Yeah, it means some tough sacrifices. A hopeful future is not easy, but think of what this can offer you. It's a literal gateway to opportunities you won't get here." The sincerity in Travis's tone, coated with insistence was hard to ignore. "Son, I fear if you look the other way on this, something like this won't come along for you. I never had a chance to make a better life for you than the one we got, but you got a chance to lift us from here and secure a comfortable future. Parents want the best for their children, and I want you to have it better than what I had to offer you."

That one stung. Mikell sat silently for a moment. "Pops...I will think about it. I'll make the decision soon. I want you to know, that I hear you. I don't want to do this, but that's not me saying I won't. I get it, and I don't know if I want it, but I see you believe it's worth it."

Travis smiled. "You got your head in the game on the court, that's for damn sure. Just gotta hope you got your head in the game of life too. I don't want to be cliche, but those shots you don't take....you will miss them all."

"Pops, if I gotta hear another basketball dad joke, I'm going to toss that letter in the trash" - Mikell said jokingly.

Travis got up and patted his son on the shoulder. "Good man...now go shower while we still got the hot water running...ya need it." - he said with a wink and walked away. That man had a way with words...

***

Mike Cassidy reread the letter dozens of times. Full scholarship to World Leadership Prep, damn near guaranteed as a starter on the basketball squad. A squad that probably needed help real bad if they tried to pull in a kid from the BNBL finals. A knock on his door broke him from his stupor.

"Yeah.." - said Mike without looking up. He did cast a glance when his door opened. Ann Cassidy's smiling face peeked in.

"You good Mikey? You've been in here for 2 hours. I usually hear you roaming around, it's been dead silent in here. Thought you were asleep. Feeling ok?" - said Ann with a hint of concern on her face, softened with a smile.

"Yeah, fine mom. Did you need anything? What did I forget?"

"Easy tiger, just making sure you are good. You are in a serious concentration daze here. Never knew you to be so serious about homework.

"Not homework, something else." - Mike said. He wanted to be subtle, but he needed to talk to someone about Lancing's invitation to World Leadership Prep. Any conversation with his father would likely end in a pointless argument, and Eric....well, he hasn't had a logical, brotherly conversation with his older sibling in years. Eric's mentality was that of a reckless, negligent, stubborn child. Mike felt like the older sibling in most interactions with him.

He pushed the letter over towards Ann as she pulled up a chair by the foot of his bed. Without bothering to ask what it was, she picked up the papers. Mike waited patiently, trying to read the expression on her face. Her face showed nothing through the first page but started to light up visibly by the time she reached the second page. Another minute that felt like an hour passed as Mike waited for any response. Ann was the type to get the full picture first, except when it came to Eric, she refused to see the full picture there. When she was done reading, she set the letter down and looked up.

"Well...what do we need to do to get this going?" - she asked bluntly with a glowing smile. "This is wonderfully unexpected."

"Whoa...who sad anyone was going to do anything about this at all? I'm just reading it over" - Mike said defensively.

"Over...and over....and over. I just read through it in under 3 minutes, you've been here staring at these pages for hours. You can probably recite it from memory by now! If you were not seriously considering it, I doubt it would have been anything you even finished reading." - Ann crossed her arms and tipped her head. "You remember who you are talking to here, Mikey? Your mother can read you like a book. I know

46

when you are serious and when you aren't before you recognize it about yourself."

"Every mother says that. " - Mike said in response. He knew that was a bull shit comment. Some of his friends had mothers that resented their very birth. Wouldn't know their kid was dealing with something if they came home with a severed limb. He knew how lucky he was, and in some ways, it was very annoying to be this transparent to anyone, even if it was the woman who brought him into the world.

"I know it sounds like a great deal, full ride and all buy, let's be real, this upends my whole life. Changes up every routine I got. Dad's always on me about getting a part-time job, this will ixnay that in a minute."

"So now what your father expects or wants from you is suddenly of importance? Crazy how convenient this timing is! But seriously Mike, however, this fell to you, you understand this is a blessing right? Prestigious schools, especially in Boston, open every door and window imaginable to the future." - Ann said more seriously after her opening quip.

"Everything I know, all the things I'm familiar with, everything I give a crap about, it's here in Southie. It's at my school, it's at my gym. This is a preppy school with a herd of nerds who probably couldn't drop a layup, looking to stack their team by pulling in kids who they saw advance to the BNBL finals. " - He choked back the rest. That was not a memory he wanted to bring up if he didn't have to. The nightmares and regret of even being there were enough of a burden.

"You're right. You would be pulled away from your school and from sharing classes with your friends. You would be leaving your basketball team. You would be jumping into a situation that is completely new to you. It would be full of sacrifices just to open doors to the very future that your family needs." - Ann put her hand up to her lips, almost regretting what she said. "I didn't mean it as it sounded. It's your life, but you know that as your mother I want to push you in the direction to be the very best version of yourself. I know your heart Mike, and I know that as much as you like to hide behind your carefree veneer, I know you are not as morally flawed as you pretend. I have always taught you that it's perfectly fine to push someone to do the obviously right thing if it's not something they can see as the right thing."

Mike's face expressed confusion, but he knew what she was saying. He adopted the facade of rolling with the punches long ago, but he had never stopped seeking to have his mother feel happy and secure about her future. She knew how concerned she was about his father's health, mental and physical, as well as what her twilight years would look like. He never stopped being scared for Eric's health and life, even though Eric made it abundantly clear that his family's concerns were not shared. Mike never stopped wanting to make his father proud of him. It's for all these reasons that Mike was not outright dismissing this unexpected opportunity.

"Look, I don't want to pressure you. If you don't choose to do this, you won't, and I know no one will convince you otherwise. But you do know that this is a fresh start. You keep trying to run away from that hideous BNBL conclusion. You blame yourself, and as I told you many times now, that is senseless. But you and I both know that at this point in your life you might be tempted to push the reset button. As far as what you'd be leaving behind....it will be the classrooms, the questionable lunch options in the cafe, and the rotten-smelling bathrooms full of unflushed toilets and pot smoke. You got your friends' numbers and addresses. You are still going to see everyone you always see, know everyone you know now, and hang with most of your same crew...and hopefully some new friends. You get to branch out. You get to step into something new and make it your own. You get to distance yourself from the past. You tell me you wouldn't want that right about now? When an angel knocks at your door, you best answer my friend." - Ann rose and pushed the chair back into place. "Anytime you want to talk...you let me know. But...I know you, and I know you will make the right choice for you, for us, and for your future."

Ann smiled and messed Mike's hair up a bit. She then headed out of his room.

"Ma..." - Mike called out. Ann opened the door and turned to look at him. "I have an important question for you...how in the hell do you know what the men's room at school smells like??"

Ann let a light laugh escape, then grinned, shrugged her shoulders, and headed out of the room. Leaving Mike to stare down at the letter again.

***

Lancing had enough to do today. The constant phone calls were a normal thing at this time of year but today was ridiculous. He couldn't put the damn phone down to focus on what he was trying to do. With every call and the people stopping by his office at a nearly constant rate today, this was turning into a wash of a day. He had actual basketball matters to think about, plays to draw up, starting positions to consider, and strategies to chart. Would have been better if he just called out sick, and then did this in peace on his day off. The phone rang yet again.

"Jesus Christ! What more can.....Hello, coach Lancing..." - His heart suddenly calmed. "Yes, this is him. I'm glad to hear from you." There was a long pause. "That's great...when can you come in for a chat.

I'll set up some time and make sure the academic advisors are available."

Finally, something was going right today...

Chapter 7

Mikell's first day was quiet and uneventful. After a pretty bland meeting with the guidance counselor, he was assigned a short-term school guide, a short Indian boy named Patesh who volunteered to show new students around. Mikell felt odd and out of place already, made only more awkward by the fact that he was also a towering giant following the soft-spoken but quick-paced junior around the school. Patesh may have volunteered for this gig, but he was sure a little too eager to get it done and over with.

Mikell absorbed as much as he could, resisting the urge to drown out Patesh by slipping his earbuds on discreetly and letting his guide say what he needed to and point at all the right things. Mikell was sure he could figure things out on his own. He wasn't looking to impress anyone in the halls, he didn't know anyone at the school and he was perfectly capable of finding both bathrooms and classrooms. But throughout the walk-around, he seemed to not encounter a gym.

Eventually, his curiosity got the better of him and he feigned a cough to get Patesh to pause and turn around.

"And the gym..." - said Mikell, trying not to sound abrasive in his tone.

"Yes...the gym, we passed that a ways back. I thought you saw. We can circle back around after." - Patesh said, then continued his rehearsed tour speech and brisk walk.

Mikell almost regretted asking. How the hell did he miss the gym? Eventually, he would come to realize that it was because there were no windows from the gym to the inside of the school building, just a door. The door read "PE/Wellness" on it in bolded but relatively small letters, and it looked like the door to a janitor closet. The giveaway should have been the long stretch of the wall without any doors or windows pointing anywhere. Mikell felt foolish for not picking up on it.

Patesh did in fact circle all the way around the school and led Mikell back to the obscure door and pointed at it with his extended hand. Mikell took that as a sign and opened the door, stepping inside. For a facility this needlessly obscured, this was a seriously dope gym. It stretched the length of two full-sized courts, with rims along the walls, alongside the primary court. The floors glistened with a glow of a recent shine-up job and struck Mikell as a place not used often enough. The gym was generally empty, save a couple of figures on the other side.

One figure raised his head from the mini huddle in the far corner and looked in Mikell's direction. He raised his arm in the air. Mikell couldn't quite tell if that was meant to indicate a "Welcome" or a "get the fuck outta here, son" gesture. Narrowing his eyes Mikell tried to focus on the features of the man with his arm up and thought it resembled coach Lancing. At that moment he heard Patesh speaking.

"Look good? It's not the most interesting part of the building, let's get down to the music area and the library. Then I'll show you the lunchroom."

Semi-unwillingly, Mikell pulled himself away from the gym door and let it slowly shut. He adjusted his bag and turned back to see Patesh heading down the hall with small but unexpectedly fast steps. Mikell followed. After showing him the rest of their destinations, Mikell began wondering when he would actually have to head to class. He tried to take a few steps to catch up to Patesh who, as usual, was multiple steps ahead of him. Patesh swung left abruptly and walked through the open door of the guidance office.

Mikell followed him inside. They passed a desk where a secretary was helping out a tall kid at the counter, straight through a short hallway with a few offices, some empty, some with people feverishly filling out paperwork on their desks. They took a sharp left and entered the biggest of the corner offices. It was almost too big to fit in the cramped hallway area. Patesh stood in front of the man behind the desk, who rose, adjusted his suit, and stuck his hand out to Mikell.

"Principle McCaullife, this is Mikell Sharp, he is new, I know you like to meet all of the new students."

"Yes sir, well aware of the legend of the BNBL! Welcome! Coach Lancing is pretty stoked to have you join us. He pushed hard for you. Glad you made the choice. How did one of your fellow basketball stars do in showing you around?"

Patesh looked at the floor. Mikell glanced in his direction surprised. "For real??"

"Lights out three-point-machine right here, and the humblest of them all! Patesh...you didn't share your prowess I see. This gentleman will be your teammate, you really should have spoken up."

Patesh looked up and shrugged. "Not what I was doing here sir, just showing him around the place like I'm tasked to do."

McCaullife nudged Patesh with his elbow. "The unassuming thing suits you on the court, but you don't have to be so silent but deadly around your teammates, or future ones anyway. This guy is only going to help us stack our quietly growing roster of a championship team. We are taking a chance on some newbies from different districts. Yeah, some say it's not the most ethical thing, and you gotta stick to your regional kids for stars, but I believe you need to get a little dirty when you are digging for gold. And if the means scooping up a future star from a heated rival, so be it. Anyhow, welcome again, Mikell. Make sure you catch up with Coach Lancing when you can. Look forward to tryouts and the season!"

"Yes sir..." - Mikell paused. "....thanks."

He headed out of the office led by Patesh. As they made their way out of the guidance office, Patesh quickly turned and said: "That's the tour. Questions?"

Mikell thought he'd get in a few. He nodded toward Patesh. "Point guard?"

"Nah...I'm a two. Would play point but, I like to shoot too much." - Mikell sensed the sarcasm as he caught a smirk slip in and come off Patesh's face breaking his otherwise deadpan joke delivery.

"And, umm....rival team? What did he mean, rival?" - Mikell asked referring to McCaullife's comment a minute ago.

"Oh, that...well...he is a Southie boy, born and bred. Given your recent history...he sees Dorchester as rivals now." - Patesh said.

"Great..." - Mikell thought sarcastically.

Patesh checked time on his FitBit, then pulled up his phone and swiped a couple of times, then tapped a few.

"Looks like you got Science, might as well get you over there, jump right into things. Faster you find the flow of this river the faster you're moving along with it, my father always told me." Patesh paused, then looked up to Mikell and nodded to follow him.

Mikell started to walk. The bell rang and doors to classrooms started to open as kids headed out for their break between periods. Mikell looked around. To some degree, he was hoping to see some faces of color, though no matter what he would see would offer him enough comfort for this mirror funhouse world of what he was used to. This might have been a terrible decision. Why the hell did his conscience have to push him to try to please Pops. This responsibility shit was going to be a life-downer. The thoughts were shaken from his head quickly, though as he passed two kids talking in the hallway. Patesh nodded to one of them, as the other nodded back. The other....his face... it's one Mikell recognized and his heart sped up about five times the speed. "What the actual fu...."

***

Mike was trying to just focus on the next minute of his day. The events of that morning were still so raw, and he had no damn idea what was going on with Eric. He had been at the school for just a couple of weeks, school work was enough of a burden. Basketball tryouts were coming soon, and for all, he knew he would be back home learning about a death in his family. Though in some ways, Eric had been gone for a long time. His shell just showed up every once in a while and did random shit around the house. Like a drone, unspeaking, uncaring, and prone only to cause problems where it went.

Mike tolerated Asher, with his snippy attitude and demeaning mouth mostly because he actually liked Mike and treated him fine, plus he befriended Mike on his third day and was the first person to do so. He was an aspiring baller in his own right, though had only made the team as a reserve. Mostly, he was a racist, ill-tempered kid who Mike would normally not hang around if he could help it, or even keep in casual company. But, he seemed to be in Asher's good graces, so he would bite his tongue and stand his company...for now.

Asher was a big talker. It's like he enjoyed hearing himself speak a bit too much. This morning was no different. The second they got out of class, Asher was already talking. Mike didn't know Asher's circle of friends but he gathered that most of them were not from the school. He was a bright enough kid, which is especially surprising considering his social inaptitudes. Asher just went on and on, Mike hearing his words, but his mind was in too much of a mess.

He tried to shift his attention to just glancing around the halls. Something about the people shuffling by on their way to class was strangely calming to him. At the same time, he knew so few of these faces that finding one he knew to draw his mind in a more positive direction would have been all but impossible. Faces floated along as he walked to the symphony of Asher's random yammering. Suddenly Mike stopped. Coming down the hall was a face that made him do a double-take. He knew this face...he knew it well. His mind was not in a place where he could rationally place it anywhere he knew, but he knew it. He tried to gear his mind to figure out where he knew this face from. And then...

"Shit...can the universe fuck with me harder today!?" he asked to no one in particular, only half realizing he said it out loud. Walking down the hall, shuffling along behind a much shorter and faster kid, was the face that snapshot into his memory as the face that turned to look at the crowd before the BNBL chaos. The bad call. The reaction that spawned the madness that gave him nightmares to this day. He remembered no other faces from the BNBL finals, except this one. That day traumatized him and many others, and this is the face he associated with all of it. Though of course....the real cause that sparked all the flame was a bad call. A foul that was not committed and Mike knew it.

But that face. How is that face in these hallways? Is this some sick setup? Cosmic level mind-fucking. He was recruited to this school for his basketball skills...so that must mean this kid was too...

"Shit!" - Mike said out loud, far louder than he anticipated.

"What?" - Asher asked.

"That kid from the riot, the drama queen who sparked the shit that went down at BNBL...he's here..." - Mike let out as he watched the kid pass several feet away from him across the hall. Then he thought better of airing his anger to Asher. The kid was black and Asher already had a questionable taste for any skin color that wasn't his own. Mike swallowed hard and followed the kid walking down the hall.

***

Mikell sat at the lunch table and pulled out his paper bag, digging out his turkey and cheese sandwich, his childhood favorite. He heard the buzzing of the lunchroom around him, full of people, and there he sat at a long table on his own. Probably for the best. He didn't exactly have the sense that he was accepted or wanted here. Coach Lancing was probably a basketball nerd who scoped him out and lured him to the school to be a part of his squad. The fewer connections he made here, the more closely he'd still feel about his ties to his Dorchester school. If everything went to shit, he had a place he knew to be familiar to go back to. Pops will be pissed though...

He tried his best to enjoy his sandwich. This was a pretty typical lunch for him, which wasn't much of a problem because it was also one of his favorites. Today, it didn't taste appealing at all though. Might be the smell of the burgers, chicken fingers, pizza, and every other tempting aroma that surrounded him. It occurred to him that this was probably unusual for cafeteria food, but he wasn't going to argue it.

His thought of sweet smells was interrupted by a kid that put his tray down in front of him and plopped down across the table. Mikell glanced to his sides instinctively but only found that the kid sitting in front of him was the only one that seemed to be joining. Regardless of intent, Mikell was in no headspace for lunch company.

"Turkey right? Any good? I find that store-bought stuff to be fucking gross myself. Sliced up and overproduced. But I got some high eating standards I guess. Gotta keep fit for hoops, you know? I mean, yeah, you obviously know. That's what you are here for right? No judgment, you just look at the part of the coach's pet project. I guess he thinks his squad ain't good enough to cut it, so he brings in outside help. I mean, we'll take the help, but you gotta not be so emotional, the coach doesn't like that. Says emotions belong on the theater stage. I agree." - The kid rattled off everything hardly taking a breath in between sentences.

Mikell stared at him. "I was invited to come, yeah. Who are you? What does getting emotional have to do with me?"

"My bad...Asher Flannigan. Team's future starting 2-guard. Just gotta land a few more shots than curry man this year and I'm in. And the emotions thing, well I mean we all know about the BNBL finals...got others who are from that game too. Heard the riot stories on the news. Heard some Dorchester kid didn't like a foul call and snapped." - Asher said with a smirk.

"You heard the stories wrong." - Mikell answered bitterly.

"Oh yeah? My bad...I guess I'll have to check with my friend then. He has some pretty good authority on what did and didn't happen out there that day." - Asher grinned.

"Whatever man. If your friend was one of the rioters maybe you should check with the cops instead. Lemme eat." - Mikell said dismissively.

"Nah, he was on the court with you and your Dorchester hood friends." - Asher snapped.

Mikell glared at Asher for a moment, then scanned the cafe for possible faces to recognize from the game. Not that this was an event he cared at all to remember the details of, but he knew he'd never forget it.

"Looking for a familiar face? I'm sure you'll see a lot of it seeing as you'll be on the same team soon. Don't worry, we care about the team winning more than who is on it. If we have to tolerate your kind then..."

Mikell slammed his fist on the table, drawing the attention of people around him. Asher put his hands up. "One team, one goal bro...don't get hot!" Recognizing the attention around him Asher piled on. "Just welcoming you to the school, good luck at tryouts. Try not to diva it up too much if you break a nail from a pass."

Mikell stood up. He knew to keep reserved but he recognized that his size would be a point of intimidation and he might as well use it since this big-mouthed clown didn't seem to be going away quickly enough.

Asher smiled. "Sit, sit my man. You are just tired. Jetlagged flying over here from Africa. Must be rough. Don't worry, you're fine right here in civilization. Boston is very first world."

Mikell's cool was down to about 5% and he was trying to hold back from doing something that would set off a chain of events that he knew would bring nothing but trouble. Asher got up, oblivious to the fact that the looks were now cast at him for his comments, and backed away slowly, hands raised in the air.

"Don't shoot, Mr. Dorchester. We only shoot on courts here. You understand? We use words here in first-world schools. We'll have the welcome wagon ready at tryouts. See you there, drama queen."

Mikell realized people were staring so he adjusted himself and sat back down. He expected friction coming to a mostly white school in this part of town but in the middle of the first day, from some racist Irish prick, that came far faster than he would have predicted.

**

"The look on his face though...oh he was fuckin bullshit with me, guy. I dropped a whole lot of lines on his ass. Or are those called bars? Isn't that what they call it in rap battles? Or is that where his kind belong and enjoy living behind?" - Asher gushed.

"Why the fuck did you even go talk to him?" - Mike felt like dropping his head in his hands. He should have kept his mouth shut about knowing the kid from BNBL. "You just stirring up shit for no reason. Fuck...I don't have it in me today to deal with more crap."

"All good man, all good!" Asher slapped him on the back. 'He doesn't know it came from you."

"Sure, not till he sees me at tryouts. My face will stand out to him just like he did to me. This is unnecessary pressure to add to the pile of shit that is my day already." - Mike frowned.

"Oh, he better recognize and know his place. Or we'll make him look like shit and Coach will reconsider putting him on the squad. Shit, we can make him want to not be on the team either. We got Patesh and Ron, that's as much "representation" as our team needs." - Asher beamed. "He does anything to you, I got your six, brother."

That last word clicked another memory of this morning and Eric's state in Mike's mind. "Your bi idea is to start shit that you then have to back me up on? That sounds like great help, I'll pass. Do me a favor man, don't start shit on someone else's behalf, especially mine. You're as helpful as Ralph Wiggum." He could tell by Asher's blank stare that he didn't get the reference and was a bit sour about his efforts earlier not being appreciated.

"Whatever...I gotta bounce, I'll see you at tryouts. Bring your game, can't let the diva get your starting spot."- Asher just couldn't help but take the parting shot.

Chapter 8

Mikell did not feel any more friction his first day, in fact, things were pretty smooth. When the final bell rang, Mikell tried to make his way back to the gym. The halls were quite a bit like a maze to someone walking through them the first time. Transferring to another school after the school year had started could have been a burdensome idea, to begin with, but having to try out for a team at the end of your first day, was just the cherry on top of a rough day.

Then again, this is the reason he joined the school, to begin with. If it wasn't for basketball, Lancing would have never approached him, he would have never had Pops convince him against every one of his instincts that this was a good way forward, and he sure as shit wouldn't be here. But here he was...so it was time to give this school what they recruited him for.

Finally locating the door, Mikell entered the gym. The sign for the locker room was pretty obvious so he headed that way. Mikell changed in the locker room, but shoved all his things into his backpack instead of in any of the dozens of open lockers, and kept his head down, avoiding anyone else who might have wandered in. He cautiously stepped out into the gym and dropped his backpack a few feet away from the locker room door. He found multiple rows of basketball-filled racks not far from him and picked up one from the top rack and slowly dribbled it out to mid-court.

About a dozen kids were running layups and firing up jump shots, though hardly any conversation or banter occurred between them. Clearly, the spirit of competition was in the air, and while most of these kids would be teammates in a few days, right now, it was warfare for a spot on the squad. Mikell stretched his limbs and dribbled up to the hoop. He warmed up with a few basic layups, glancing around apprehensively at the other kids. He saw Patesh shooting free throw after free throw from the free-throw line. The best Mikell could tell, he nailed every single one.

Mikell continued his warmup, gradually increasing the intensity of his drives and firing up turnaround jumpers. He then saw Coach Lancing and two other older guys in similar attire enter the gym. They didn't seem to be paying much attention to who was on the court, just busily discussing something amongst themselves.

Deciding to focus back on the game, Mikell turned to take another run at the basket and bumped directly into another player across.

"Oh...my bad..." - Mikell said, looking up at the kid. His voice caught in his throat as the face he saw took him straight back to the BNBL finals. "....you...what the fuck are you..."

"Surprise, surprise, big man" - teased Asher who just entered the court. "Told ya my buddy had the authority to speak on you being a drama queen"

Mikell never took his eyes off of the face that he would not forget. "So this is some kind of joke then?"

"Surprised to see you play ball here. With your broadway future calling. Or do you think you are an automatic here because of your kind thinking of their ballers?" - said the kid facing Mikell.

Mikell squeezed the basketball so hard he thought for a second he would actually deflate the thing. He nudged the kid with it in the chest. "You think you are gonna outplay me for it? Couldn't do it in BNBL, had to have the zebra give you a ride to the free-throw line with a bullshit call. How much do you and your little Irish mafia bitches stick into his pocket for that favor?"

"We were handing you your asses as it was, why would we waste money bribing? What are you smoking over there in your Dorchester hood?"

"Gonna be smokin' your ass in a minute unless you back up outta my grill!" - Mikell snapped.

"Oh shit, Cassidy. I know you ain't gonna let that Dorchester savage talk to you like that!" - flaunter

Asher from the side, inching closer to the brewing conflict.

Hearing the racist jab triggered Mikell to turn and chest pass the ball in his hands right at Asher's face. Realizing what was happening Asher tried to get his hands up, but the quickly flying ball was true enough to its target, mostly beating Asher's arms in speed, catching him in the eye, cheek, and ear. Asher recoiled, grabbing his face.

Before Mikell got any satisfaction a hard shove sent him recoiling to the floor. He turned to see that Cassidy kid stepping toward him. Fire in his eyes, Mikell burst back to his feet and lunged at the kid.

***

Mike wasn't exactly Asher's biggest fan, but he had his back in Asher's own stupidly misguided way so he didn't stand around while his friend got nailed across the face with a basketball. He quickly reacted by shoving the assaulting party down to the floor. Mike figured this would not go without retaliation, but it came far quicker than he expected.

The black kid was up on his feet coming at him within two seconds, and Mike was not entirely prepared for the force with which the kid pushed him and stumbled backward two steps before falling hard on his back on the court with the black kid on top of him. Mike covered up his face only to have a fist nail him in the top of his head and another snuck in under the chin.

Mike wasn't going to just lay and take a beating, so with this other arm, he threw a hard, direct punch to the kid's gut, then did it again, and again. The kid backed up in pain, allowing Mike to stretch his other hand out, wrap it into a fist, and nail his attacker on the bridge of his nose. He felt warm blood splatter across his own face. The kid drew back, but only for a moment, and descended on him again. Mike's hand went up over his face again. His legs moved up instinctively with his knee accidentally finding the black kid's nuts, which quickly subdued the attack.

With one final grab, the kid grabbed Mike's jersey and pulled on it. Mike heard tearing as it was being pulled away from his body. It was just an old raggedy no-sleeve tee, but it was one of Mike's favorites. This move stung for sure.

It was at that moment that the rest of the team, including Asher, jumped in to separate the two fighters. Mike could hear Lancing's voice yelling at them to break it up and at the other boys to separate them from any further fighting. The kid held on to Mike's shirt tightly, so while he was moaning in pain from being kneed in the groin, he was definitely taking that shirt with him in the pull-apart.

Asher, Patesh, and three other boys finally dragged Mike from underneath his attacker, resulting in a completely ripped shirt and a bruised ego. Lancing was between them now, hands stretched out in some kind of old-school effort to separate them.

"Keep them apart, damn it! First day...not even ....tryouts, and already! I want these two in my office right now." - Lancing yelled. "Get 'em in there!"

Some of the boys were confused. The coach's office was constantly being moved from across the building to next to the gym. They stared at him with dumbfounded looks until he finally pointed across the gym to a door that read "Coach Lancing" on it. Mike gathered that this location must have been new.

***

The boys at the tryouts led both Mike and Milkell to Coach's office, realizing at the door that they would have to let them go, and there was a good chance they'd go at it again. Coach held the door open, giving Mikell a stern look and whipping his head in the direction of the inside of his office as if to say "get your ass in there!"

Mikell ripped away from the grips that were holding him, adjusted his shirt and shorts, wiped his nose, and stepped in. He saw a couch against the wall and sat on the far end of it. Mike Cassidy was in there next sporting a bruise on his forehead and a shiner across his cheek. Coach yelled to the other boys to keep staying warm and shut the door behind him.

"Sit your ass down Cassidy!"

Chapter 9

Coach Lancing shut the door, and grabbed a towel on a corner hook, wiping his forehead with it. He turned and walked around his desk, moving his chair out with his foot, then slowly sat down in it.

"I gotta be honest with you guys, I knew this would happen. To the core of my damn soul, I knew that bringing the two of you face to face, given your history, and the shit that you both had to live through because of what happened, I truly, genuinely knew that once you met again, it would not be an easy experience for either of you. But holy shit did I not think it would take under two minutes to escalate."

Mikell and Mike glanced in each other's direction. Seeing that the other one was also looking, both quickly diverted their gaze. Mikell's eyes shifted to the coach, Mike's eyes down to the floor.

"Look, I could sit here and tell you that I am sorry that I did not tell you that we recruited the other one too, how we need to get past this, how with you two on the squad, this team stands a great chance of shining this season. I could butter you up with all the classic fairy tale dreams and aspirations of glory and dazzle you with empty rhetoric that I have no way of proving, but I've never been a man ...or a coach, who takes particular delight in insulting people's intelligence, especially that of the people who I expect to entrust to my leadership on the court."

Lancing looked from one boy to the other and continued: "This is not a therapy session, we won't sit here and work on everyone's feelings. We are not going to go some B movie route and have you settle it in a one-on-one game against one another. I am just going to tell you the God's honest truth. And that truth is that not letting the two of you know about each other was very intentional, as was working hard to recruit both of you here. If you think the decision was only mine and that the leadership of this school was reveling at the idea of uniting two polarizing figures like yourselves on the same team, drawing that level of scrutiny to this school on the whisper of a dream that we will improve our standing, you would be dead wrong."

Lancing rose from this chair. "There was a lot of convincing, and frankly, ass-kissing and over-justification to people who wouldn't know how to dribble a ball if they had 6 arms and foot-wide hands, eager only for the boosting of the school's name and state exposure. Shit, they would have settled for a team that doesn't suck! Everyone saw the BNBL, even the most basketball-inept around here watch the damn news. The coverage was not lost on them and your faces were all too familiar. That's why it would be pretty fucking discouraging if all of the effort that went into bringing in multiple top-notch players to this school to beef up our squad with BNBL stars, just to have the entire experiment scrapped on the first day, because a hyper-sensitive Dorchester kid and Pennywise-ass from Southie over here, decided to start tryouts with a fight."

He paused, clearly for dramatic effect. "Now, word of this will likely make it back to McCauliffe before tomorrow morning, and if you want to see an unreasonable man bark at the moon, you just wait till he gets it in his head that he was convinced into an instant failure with your recruitment. So hear me when I tell you this: I know you took some hard chances to make the leap here for you both. You had every reason to refuse, toss the letters I handed you, and go about your lives like this never happened. You would have been with your friends, you would have been with your teams, and you would have been a shitton closer to home. But you made the hard choice, and here you are. All those sacrifices, all of those sleepless nights of tossing and turning, thinking about how this decision could impact your life or the lives of your families...it can all go away." Lancing snapped his fingers, triggering both Mikell and Mike to look up at him.

"Now, when McCauliffe hears about the fight, and rest assured there is zero chance that he doesn't, he will trigger some formal Kabuki theater, grandstanding, morally insulting bullshit response. On one of your earliest days in the school, the entire reason you decided to come here, to open doors for yourselves and your families by leveraging your unfairly granted basketball talents will...." Lancing simulated a whooshing sound. "...just like that."

Mikell and Mike glanced at each other again, this time caring less that the other was looking too.

"The only way we have a chance to bypass this is to get ahead of it. If I cut McCaullife's nonsense with a harsh enough seeming plan, a jarringly strict way to cut this off at the knees, I suspect it will stun him into letting me handle the situation myself, rather than him butting in. And we will not handle it in a parking lot brawl, we will not handle it in an unnecessarily violent scrimmage, or a shouting match. We are going to go the route of an ultimatum."

Both boys raised their eyebrows: "If this is your way of expressing how badly you don't want to be here, then you very clearly wasted your time, mine, and this school's in agreeing to come here. So I'm guessing that isn't your goal. Point blank, you two will be teammates unless you have suddenly lost all of your basketball prowess. You will be playing together which requires that you foster comradery. Call it an uncomfortable alliance of convenience. You don't have to be best friends or even buddies, but you must be teammates. If I can't expect that from each of you, then there is no reason for you to be at this school. So before we get you court-ready, we are going to get you teammate-ready. Think of this as your first evaluation, one that you must pass in order to progress to a member of this squad."

Lancing had now circled around his desk and sat on the front of it looking from Mike to Mikell and back again.

"So here is the deal: until you two can work out an amicable relationship, I cannot have you on my squad, and if I cannot have you on my squad, McCaullife will send both of your asses back to where you came from....and probably mine too for vouching so hard for such an immediate and magnificent failure. It will be an ugly experience for us all, so I don't know about you, but I'd rather avoid it. Therefore, you two are going to learn how to be a united front off the court, and then on it. After school, there is an hour-long study hall, optional for students. More people than you think to use that time because it is free of home distractions like noises, nagging parents, video games, and younger siblings. You two are to meet there and help each other out with homework, then, you two need to report to the courts and run basic drills. Just you two. McCaullife takes off by that point so until he wisens up to your post-study hall activities, you are good on that front. Just remember, this plan may be optional for others, but for you, it ain't! Work out the conflicts, squash whatever crap you need to because this is an exercise of your judgment, and my trust in that you two are smarter than the two idiots who brawled at tryouts today and will now make the best out of this opportunity. Now...my throat is begging for some water, but I need to know...are we clear on the conditions?"

Mikell and Mike glanced at each other again. Their looks did not express any form of excitement at the idea of working together. Mike knew that this is something that no matter how badly he didn't want to do, he knew what was going on at home...or at least he hoped he knew, and there would be no way he could live with himself if he put this on his poor parents too now, of all times.

Mikell dreaded the idea of telling Pops that he got kicked out from the opportunity Pops so readily advised him into taking. There were a lot of conversations he could bring himself to talk to Pops about, but this would not be one of them.

It seemed like working together to work through the bullshit will be their only viable option. For whatever it may bring, this would have to be the way it goes. Each boy just hoped that the other would not push his buttons enough for them to need to stop giving a shit about the consequences of their actions.

Mikell looked at Lancing and nodded. Mike stared at the floor. "Hey...Southie, did I lose ya? I know I talked a lot but did you drift off to neverland? I'm sorry, I am more of a yelling play on the court guy, never was one for dramatics. Don't judge me too harshly there, resident expert." Lancing turned to Mikell who took a second to catch the "drama" zinger thrown at him and shook his head. Lancing winked. Mikell rolled his eyes. "While you are rolling your eyes, let me know how that brain of yours looks."

Lancing turned back to Mike. The kid was visibly stifling a laugh after the joke at Mikell's expense. "You seem awake to me...am I going to get some consent, a refusal....a grunt, maybe? Hell, I'll take any form of communication, it doesn't even have to be English."

Mike immediately felt a sense that he didn't know about Coach Lancing before. This guy had a way with words....and dad jokes. Either way, he just turned this hostile, awkward conversation into a bit of a comedic hang-out.

"Yeah...I can make it work." Mike said suppressing a smile.

"Oh, you can both make it work...Will you make it work is the thing I'm most curious about. Glad we agree. Hope this was not all worth nothing. Now get your asses outta here and head home. We will try you out at make-up. Get to study hall tomorrow. I'll be seeing you around, gentlemen."

Chapter 10

The walk from Lancing's office was awkward and silent. Mike and Mikell walked straight past the boys running drills, hardly casting a glance in their direction. When they neared the locker room entrance, they heard Lancing's voice in the background trying to get the guys together to get the tryouts moving along. Both felt that they fucked things up, but resented the other for being the catalyst that they perceived for the confrontation.

Mikell reached the locker room doors first and pushed the door open to enter. He did not hold the door for Mike who, by the time he was near it, had the door essentially shut in his face. He caught it with inches to spare and pushed it open angrily, biting his tongue. He did not need any more crap today.

As the cruel twist of fate would have it, it turned out that the lockers they chose to use were across the walkway from each other. They sat in the most awkward of quiet and changed back into their street clothes. The outside of the building was just behind the far wall, and it seemed that the rain was picking up again. Mikell was not looking forward to his bus trip back to Dorchester but was more than ready to leave the building.

Mike was trying to get dressed quickly. Walking in alongside Mikell was weird enough, he wanted to be sure to be ready to head out before him. Still biting his tongue his thoughts drifted to Eric. He thought it was very odd that he heard nothing at all. Then again, perhaps it was a good sign. If something awful ended up happening, his parents would have sent word to summon him from school by now.

On the other hand, he could see his mother wanting to get her bearings on the tough situation, before worrying her youngest son about whatever they would have to deal with as a family. This day certainly had all the makings of a shitshow already, so Mike was bracing himself for the worst.

He dug into his bag once he was dressed and pulled out his old iPod. He didn't know the school's policy on phones so he kept that home, though he regretted it now. He fumbled for his headphones, pressing the play button in the process, setting off "Shotty Shane" by Digga D. Without the headphones on the beat pierced the locker room, startling both boys. Mikell shot a look over to Mike who quickly fumbled to pause the music, but not before letting nearly 8 seconds of the beat drop.

Finally finding the button to shut off the music. Mike breathed an awkward sigh of relief. He didn't know why he felt embarrassed. Drill rap was music he had been digging for about 4 years now. Once he heard it he just couldn't get enough of it. Yet somehow, a white Southie kid listening to drill rap would not be appreciated by his social circles or his community. So it was relegated to an interest that he held dearly but privately. On top of everything, for this to blare across the locker room like that, with a black kid about 15 feet away, one with who he had a sore history, well that was just a different type of embarrassing.

**

Mikell was shaken from the sudden drop of a beat, jarred by the music he enjoyed coming from the music player of this obvious poser from Southie, and straight shocked that this is what the kid was listening to. Some cruel twist of fate put this kid who was at the center of the act that upended his mental well-being, ending up at the same school, trying out for the same basketball team, and now being forced to work run drills together. And on top of that mountain of ironic hot garbage, now it turned out he listened to the same music that Mikell loved.

Drill rap is something that Mikell's friends knew he was into, even if not all of them were. But Pops, well, he was an open-minded man in many ways, but the man could not absorb new music if it was fed to him by force through megaphones attached to his ears. And this type of music, the man would never understand, and in all likelihood be mortified by what he heard if he ever gave it an actual listen.

Mikell heard what he heard, and while he was shaken by the surprise, his first reaction was to let out a laugh. He quickly caught himself and reeled it back in. But the kid heard him. Mikell tried not to look in his direction.

"What?" - Mike asked with a harsh tone of defiance in his voice. "Too low brow of rap for your taste? Laugh it up, Dorchester. You can get back to spinning your Boyz II Men CDs back in the hood soon."

The kid's comment was meant to burn but it amused Mikell more. The kid was kind of funny without intending to be that. He smirked and shook his head. Couldn't let the Southie boy see any cordial facial expressions after all.

"Yeah...if you're struggling to talk, it's fine. I would be struggling to listen to your voice anyway." - Mike seemed unnecessarily angry about the whole thing, while the thoughts of how stupid of a thing this was to get mad about floated in his head. "If you got thoughts, keep 'em to yourself. Lancing's speech was enough for me."

Mikell felt he should respond, but every response that came to mind would have fallen flat. So at the risk of seeming cocky or stupid, he kept his mouth shut.

Mike collected his stuff and shoved it in his backpack. Casting a side glance in Mikell's direction, Mike headed for the door. He slowed as he neared the locker room door.

"After school tomorrow…" - He said, allowing the end of this sentence to trail off.

Mikell found his voice: "I know…don't have much of a choice."

"You do….you can drop out and go back to your hood school. Be fine with me. Solves a lot of issues." - Mike shot back, not turning to face his nemesis.

"Would be easier for you not to have any competition on the squad. Easier to not get shipped out of this school." The sarcasm was flowing from Mikell now…why stop? "Was considering bailing actually. But…if it makes you this miserable for me to stay, not sure I can pass up this kind of golden opportunity. I think I'll stay around."

After a pause to soak in the sarcasm and counterbalance it with his feelings of anger and concern for Eric, a topic that has not eased in his mind at all, Mike replied: "Fine, but if you don't make the squad, I hear the theater club is pretty good. Always good to have a fallback plan."

"To be or not to be, Southie, that is the question. Gonna just have to see who can ball and who joins theater, Southie. And yeah...after school tomorrow." - Mikell tried to get the last word.

"Yup...and fuck you Dorchester." - Mike wasn't letting him get the last word, so he headed for the door.

"Hey!" - Mikell called out. Mike slowed his pace. He felt provoked. "Digga D? For real?"

"Fuck off, Dorchester." - said Mike and pulled open the locker room door.

Chapter 11

Mikell struggled through his bowl of cereal the next morning. The anxiety was eating at him. One day on the court in a new school he never wanted to attend, and he somehow already got himself into some shit. He liked to tell himself that getting caught up in stupid garbage like this was beneath him, yet he somehow found himself in these annoying situations over and over again.

The damned curse of bad decisions. Unfortunately for Mikell, it carried through his family like an unshakable leach, infecting every family member in their own way. Mikell was not an only child, but his brother Reyjan had long since passed. Wrong gang, wrong place, wrong time....many wrong decisions. Mikell was only 7 back then, and while he missed his brother, they never had a relationship close enough of kinship to warrant a bond that would tie them so close as to be inseparable. Reyjan was 9 years older, and at the time of his passing, he hardly spent any time at home, always chilling with his hood buddies.

Mikell had only vague memories of his big brother, and he did feel upset because everyone around him took the loss hard. Pops was a little lighter. Mikell thought it was because he needed to be strong in order to comfort his mother (for all the good that did), but with time he began to suspect that there really was that Pops had accepted that his oldest son was a lost cause and wouldn't make it past the age of 25. Mikell wasn't sure if 16 was the age that they were prepared to lose him.

Mikell's mom, Tamara, took the loss harder than anyone. She cried for hours, lashed out in anger at Mikell and Pops, only to come apologizing later, blaming it all on her stress levels, anxiety, and depression. Mikell was too young to understand those terms, but he wanted to have a mom he could get along with. Perhaps one day they could have, but much like Reyjan's shitty decision-making got him killed, Tamara decided to forego grief and chose a route of escape. It started with way too high doses of painkillers, then went to sleep aid pills, and eventually, harder drugs.

Looking back now, he could see how a mother would want to escape the horrible reality of her child's death, even if that child was doomed in the eyes of everyone else. It was just so impossible for a mother to accept. He had been woken several times at night, some to ambulance sirens trying to revive his mother, some at Pops yelling at her to wake her up when she passed out cold. Being so young, Mikell just wanted all the yelling and craziness to go away, so he could live the happy life that he saw kids on TV living with their parents.

Sadly, that was not to be. Tamara would eventually fire up one too many hard drugs, and one morning he slept in, mostly due to being kept awake by noises at night, to find Pops closing the door to a man with a hat. Mikell still remembered the parting look of pity that the man gave him out of the corner of his eye. In some ways, Mikell was glad he slept through what must have been a horrible scene to witness. Pops sat Mikell down and explained that his mother got very sick, but she would be well now, and she would rest with the Lord watching over her from now on. To heal her, Pops said, the Lord has to hold on to her, but they would get to keep the memories. He must have forgotten that Mikell had hardly any positive memories of his mother since he was just a child of about 4 or 5, and those were fuzzy.

The loss of his son and wife would turn any man into a grieving bucket of tears, but not Pops. He had one son left, and he was going to make sure that boy got things right. Luckily, Mikell was still young and impressionable. He also had no desire to cause his family, or Pops specifically any more harm. He told himself when he turned 10 that he would be on his best behavior so that Pops, who was facing struggles at work at the time, would have no reason to shake his optimistic view of the world. Mikell admired the fact that his father would spin every negative into a positive, but he didn't admire how hard Pops was determined to guide Mikell into a better life.

Pops turned into what Mikell had heard referred to as a helicopter parent. He was sickeningly encouraging, even about things Mikell had no interest in, but he was frighteningly everpresent especially considering the balanced full-time job, and yet found a way to be there for everything. Mikell began to worry that his father never slept, or would just simply collapse from a lack of energy one day. But Pops kept going, no matter what shitstorm life brought, he was there, pushing the positivity. As Mikell got older Pops began to trust his judgment more and backed off to a degree.

Pops was always there with advice, though mostly unsolicited. Mikell figured that's just how fathers operated, and perhaps he should be thankful, but there was a part of the intrusiveness and the hovering that made this "helicopter parent" behavior not only tough to keep away from, it was suffocatingly impossible to escape. Mikell was on the verge of telling Pops to back the fuck off and let him live his life. He certainly viewed these all as bad decisions by his father who wanted to pretend that life in the hoods of Dorchester wasn't tough as hell and hopeless as shit, at least for his son. But in all fairness, Mikell was here, alive, an athlete of decently high regard...perhaps he should be thankful.

But being thankful was not on his mind when Pops plugged himself into every aspect of his life. So there Mikell sat with a hovering cereal spoon in the air wondering how he would tell Pops that he had to hang back after school today to work out differences after one day on the court at a new school Pops encouraged him to go to. He would probably spin this into a positive too, but Mikell always had a lingering feeling that every time his own bad decisions came around, informing Pops would finally be the straw that breaks the strong, positive, apparently sleep-deprived optimism machine. So every step of the way, it was pure agony to think about dropping this on him.

But he would have to tell him, and he'd have to tell him today because Pops would be wondering why he wasn't back at his expected time. Pops passed through the kitchen nodding at Mikell with a half-smile. Something was clearly on his mind. Pops made some instant coffee and then sat at the table with Mikell, taking a sip and staring at his son's eyes.

"So we made the team, I assume? Or did the white boys run circles around you and bury threes? Can't stop what you can't catch I guess." - Pops blurted out.

"Ummm..."- Mikell wrestled with whether or not to drop the truth on Pops. After such a short period of time, he was already at risk of not getting on the team, and not for his lack of skills, but because he couldn't keep his mouth shut when he probably should have. - "the best shooter out there is Indian."

Pops raised an eyebrow...."Well...didn't see that one coming but you didn't answer my question. The team...?"

"Just had tryout Pops, they gotta figure it out. Gotta hang back tonight for follow-ups. May need to for a few days." - Mikell struggled to think about moving on with his conversation. This felt like a "less is more" kind of situation.

"Well, I got no doubt you're getting on it, just don't go messin' up in the classroom, son. I want you got to succeed on all fronts. I know you want that too. I'm sure there will be reasons to consider throwing it all away. Someone will step on your toes, say the wrong thing, or nail you with a hard foul. I know it's hard to bite your tongue, really slaps your self-respect in the face, but keep a cool head and get over and past things. Just remember, your future is more important than any minor problems the present will bring."

Mikell's stomach turned. It's almost like Pops could read his problems off his face, yet was communicating it in a subtle manner, offering advice without speaking explicitly to it.

"I know Pops, don't sweat it...all good." - Mikell felt wrong for keeping it in, but this was not the time or the person to have any longer of a conversation with.

"I know son, I know. You're my levelheaded one. I am glad this old man didn't fail in one respect at least. If I leave any mark or legacy on this world, I'm glad it's you." - With that Pops picked up his coffee, got up took a sip, patted Mikell on the shoulder, and headed out of the room. Mikell heard Pops head into the living room. He put down his spoon of cereal. No appetite. Time to endure this day.

***

Mike came home to an empty house the night before, having heard very little from his parents regarding Eric. He had a couple of pop tarts for dinner and threw on his headphones. Every time he thought he heard a noise he would first quick glance at his phone for texts, then pull his earbuds out to listen for movement in the house. He sat in a dark living room, waiting to see the headlights outside. The only text he saw that night was "Stable" ....that's all...a one-word sign that Eric was alive from his father.

Mike closed his eyes and tried to sink into the drill rap beats. Even at this moment of stress, anxiety, and the unknown, Mike was simply seeking the escape of music. He would recognize that he had not checked on his surroundings in a while, four songs at a time, he would unplug and open his eyes. No blinding headlights from outside, no shuffling around the house, no sudden, startling shoulder taps from his mom or dad. He sat there alone.

Mike lost all sense of time, only keeping an idea of how long it had been through the songs he heard. He zoned out to a point of losing track of where he was. When he came to, his phone was playing a different album than the one he started. He jolted straight up and looked at his phone. It was dark outside, but the clock read only 10:48 PM. Last he knew it was just after 9. He must have fallen asleep.

The jolt made him awake...very awake. He felt like he was freakishly refreshed for some reason. He pulled the headphones off and got up to stretch his legs. His comfortable couch had a knack for being so comfortable that it punished anyone who enjoyed its comfort for too long with stinging back spasms once they got up. Mike was sad to discover he was no exception to that rule. He placed his hands on the wall of his dark house and twisted his back until he heard some satisfying cracks. He did the same with his neck.

He looked at his phone again, only to find it had only been 2 minutes. He then began to slowly pace around the room. The deprivation of light yielded him the ability to think through the goings-on in life. His mind floated back to all his greatest anxieties. He thought about the hassle he would face with his unwanted arrangement just to qualify for a basketball team that he should be a shoo-in for.

Then there is Eric's recovery. His big brother was family, but also he was a drain, financial, mental, and emotional on their parents, neither of whom deserved the fate that their older child dealt them. In many ways, they already lost their firstborn son, he was but a shell. An obnoxious, selfish zombie who kept returning to feast on their barely surviving hearts and brains.

Mike wandered the room and thought about everything. He was jolted out of his trance by a pair of headlights pointing at the house. He rushed to the window hoping to see his parents. Sadly it was just someone turning around. Noises outside drew his attention as he saw the O'Keefe brothers yelling at each other two doors down. These two butted heads more than anyone he knew, but at least they had each other and had a kinship going. Mike only wished he had that, but he would never admit it to anyone.

He checked his phone and headed to bed finding that he had been pacing for over 2 hours, and it was closing in at 1 AM. But being in bed didn't bring sleep, all it brought was more thoughts. The first ray of sunlight crept in eventually when Mike was finally on the brink of sleep. He reached for his phone and set a time for 1 hour. This was timely, as less than a minute later he was off into a long-needed doze.

The alarm nearly didn't wake him an hour later. Of all things, he heard noises in the home. It was a clacking sound, so he rolled out of bed, wiping drool from his cheek, and headed downstairs. The house was quiet and what he heard sounded almost like water dripping.

He walked into the dining room to find his mother at a computer. She had circles under her eyes, tear marks all over her face, and was busy typing in things with one finger at a time. When she saw him, she jumped. Mike put his hands up to ease her concern. She quickly used her sweatshirt to wipe her nose and eyes and waved him over. When he approached she threw her hands around him and squeezed him to the point that oxygen was starting to become an issue.

"Mom....what's going on? Where is Eric, and dad?" - Mike asked.

"Dad had to go to work, I tried to talk him out of it. I hate the idea of him driving on no sleep. Big project coming to a close in a couple of weeks he said he could not miss it. Eric is in a hospital bed. He will be ok they say...they uh...." - she hesitated. "Mike...they have him handcuffed, he is out, but handcuffed. Deemed a danger to himself and those around him."

"Shit...I mean, I get it, but it's...just hard to believe." - Mike blurted out.

"He thrashed, he kicked, he knocked out a poor nurse's tooth. She was just trying to help him. They had to sedate him." - Mom was beginning to sob but pulled herself together. It was an ugly scene, Mike, I am so glad you weren't there for it."

"I can't even imagine. What are you looking up?" - Mike nodded to the computer.

"Oh ...I.....just seeing what I can do about a dusted-off resume." - she said, sheepishly.

"Ma, you haven't worked in like 8 years... what's going on?" - Mike was starting to worry. Why now? Dad was the provider for nearly a decade and they were fine. She kept up with the house, he brought the money. It was old school, outdated, but it worked for them in a non-demeaning way.

"Eric will be forced into rehab. It's either that or jail. From his standpoint, rehab is jail. His damned addiction is his only true 'peaceful' mode of existence. He sees anything else as some kind of intrusion on his ability to live the life he views as 'great' and ....well....the costs are going to add up. Your father works too hard and simply won't be able to get another raise now until the project completes and funding for a new one comes around. So I need to do what I can." - She explained.

This all made sense to Mike, and he knew his mom would work hard wherever she landed, but the pressure this put on their family made him borderline hate his selfish prick of a brother just a little more. He almost wished that Eric would be jailed. But some part of him could hopefully be redeemed...though Mike doubted it.

"Ma, why don't you take a break. Get some sleep and a shower. I gotta head off to school, and you're not going to be functional without some rest. Let me help you to bed."

In return, he received a sob-filled hug. "Bless you, Mikey, bless you...seriously. I am not sure you can appreciate how glad your father and I are for you. I know he has been hard on you, but trust me, I know him deeper than anyone, and the talks we have had. Your dad is beyond thankful for and proud of you. At least your father and I got one thing right. Just keep going strong with your life, don't let the rest of it drag you down, ok?"

Mike felt a deep sense of shame for his current situation at his new school, but he would not mention it here. He nodded in return and walked his mother upstairs, helping her out of her sweatshirt and laying her in bed, tucking her under the covers. When she closed her eyes and fell nearly instantly asleep from utter exhaustion, he headed into the shower. He was not going to be the drain that Eric was. He would wash any of his shortcomings off him that morning, and he would revitalize himself to be the kind of son, and the kind of man his family needed right now.

Chapter 12

Mike did not need to burden his family with any more hardships. He was not stuck in this hideous situation of having to excuse being late at school perpetually, while he was not formally on a basketball team. He wondered how long Lancing would drag him and Mikell through this "bonding for teamwork" crap. In retrospect, keeping his mouth shut would have been the smart thing to do at tryouts.

So every day became a regular roundoff of fabricated excuses. The fact that his parents were under this much strain with Eric's situation and his mom was now job-hunting every day ate Mike up inside, but weirdly, it worked to his advantage. The reason for his after-school delays was not regarded with many questions, as his parents trusted that he was using the time to practice with his team.

To his surprise, Lancing largely left him and Mikell operating on their own. The plans changed from the initial impression Mike had about what was going to be occurring. He and Mikell were told to hone their court skills independently at first, then one on one against each other. They were also put on glorified janitorial duties, as they were responsible for emptying trash cans in classrooms, washing down desks, clearing boards, and assuring that the board markers were still functional before they left the classroom. They were assigned two rooms per day and had to work those together.

Their on-court interaction would have potentially been volatile, but Lancing sat in watching their one-on-one scrimmages against each other intently, while the other boys practiced on the other side of the court. Mike and Mikell both understood that any more verbal altercation would be seriously detrimental for them, but they were going to work out their agitation with each other, and the situation they put each other in during their one-on-ones. With Lancing's eyes trained upon them, they had to keep the roughness to a minimum.

Mike found Mikell extremely difficult to defend. His crossovers could snap and ankle of the fastest defender, and the height he got from his jump shot was damn near unnatural. Mike did figure out that if he pushed Mikell further from the rim, he weakened his chances. Mikell was a solid shooter, but the further from the basket he moved, the lower the shot success rate became. Both boys were sweaty and exhausted afterward, which made it more infuriating that they had to show up to do another hour of classroom cleanup.

Mikell too felt the frustration. Mike obviously figured out that pushing him further from the rim reduced his shot accuracy, so he tried to use his bigger body to power his way to the rim, catching himself on too aggressive of nature, however, knowing that the coach was staring them down.

His reach and slight height advantage were things he believed would be great weapons against Mike's outside game, but the annoyingly persistent prick just kept nailing jumpers like it was nothing. Mike would attempt to drive and pop up a fancy layup here and there, some got through, but Mikell was able to swat most of them away, sometimes with an emphatic "whack" that by sheer chance hadn't yet resulted in at least a jammed finger. Mikell had to admit though, that this kid was accurate, fast, and beyond all that, he was the type of player that when he stepped onto the court, was focused like a laser. But he did have a weak spot. Mikell could see it. If Mike was in the zone, he was a damn hard player to face, but once rattled, the stress got to him. This was clearly detrimental to him on the court.

Mikell savored exploiting this when he could, but it occurred to him several days after this discovery that if he picked up on this, players that would play against them would too. This was no longer about the competition between them. Leaving this unchecked would quickly become detrimental to the team if they were both allowed on it. He had to point it out.

***

After the first week, it seemed that Lansing lost interest in watching the two battle it out in one on one practice. He would hang by the rest of the boys and run drills, issue guidance, and engage in way too much whistle-blowing, as well as more sarcastic critiques than any human being Mikell or Mike had ever heard. It was a little strange not to be constantly supervised, by the lingering feeling of Lancing always paying attention kept the two playings hard against one another.

Mikell did see this as a chance to point out Mike's weakness. After noticing hesitation in his step, Mikell was able to snag the ball away from Mike. He looked up at his counterpart's face to see gritted teeth and mouthing of "fuck." Mikell smirked but quickly retracted finding a better sense in his actions.

"Once you break, you are dust, kid." - he jabbed.

"Ha? If I am so broken, come score on me tough-nuts." - Mike spat back.

Mikell obliged, and true to form he was able to scoot around Mike for a fake layup, then a mid-air pump fake which sent Mike jumping high into the air for a block, but it's when Mike began to give in to gravity that Mikell fired the shot. He made it, but just barely. The ball toilet balled around the rim before dropping in. Mikell would take it, but not with pride.

"Stress is a crippler, gotta tune that shit out on the court or you will break when things don't go right." - Mikell offered, trying to sound genuine.

"Thanks for the sage advice there, superstar. Give me a moment to pretend to consider its value. Done....useless. Now shut up and give me the ball." - Mike snapped back.

Mikell shrugged. "Just trying to prevent future mistakes that will cost us games. The time to get less fragile is now." He checked Mike the ball.

Mikell glanced over at Lancing who was clearly just staring at them, turning his eyes away the moment Mikell turned. Before he knew it, Mike was speeding past him on his way to the basket. Cursing himself for taking his eyes off the game, he tried to turn after him but was far too late as Mike cruised right past him for an easy layup.

"The thing fragile here is your D, big guy. Your ball." - Mike raised his eyebrows as if hinting for Mikell to back up to get the ball checked to him. Mikell did and got the ball in his hands. Before he knew it, Mike was directly in front of him. Instinctually Mikell stepped back to protect ball possession. Mike's hands waved at ball level and Mikell was forced to back up further. He tried to go to the side but Mike darted in front. He would go to his trusty crossover, but Mike was persistently too close. As Mikell backed up, Mike moved up on him, keeping the distance between them minimal. Backed to nearly the three-point arc, Mikell dodged to the side, fooling Mike to follow then pulled the other way and put up a jumper. The ball took a line drive, bouncing violently off of the front of the rim, ricocheting back in their direction, nailing Mike in the back of the leg.

Mike quickly turned as Mikell lunged for the ball to try another shot. Mike had it in his possession first and quickly darted to the opposite side of the rim. When he was far enough away, he turned to face Mikell. Mikell darted at him with his hand up in the air, stumbling a bit from his initial attempt at the loose ball. Mike stepped back and put up a jump shot that sailed right through the net, never touching the rim, producing the purest, most satisfying swoosh.

"That right there is how you bury jumpers, not whatever you just did. Fragile...yeah, like glass. I like to call it being clear-cut though. But looks like you can only dominate near the rim. Move you back, and you're useless just like your advice. Good thing you have me to point it out to you. We wouldn't want opposing teams figuring that out, would we?" - Mike delighted at being snide.

The two both turned as they heard clapping hands. "Trash talking on the court. I like it. Better than being idiots and starting fights. Been waiting on you two to start talking for a while now. You're done for the day here, go get your other responsibilities done. Come see me after." - somehow Lancing was right next to them, using some sort of ninja moves to approach while neither noticed.

***

The silence was never awkward, as Mike and Mikell typically had no desire or need to speak to each other but after interacting on the court, now not speaking just felt weird. Both split their duties in the classroom cleaning without communicating. Ironically enough they somehow inherently figured out that if one person does something in one classroom, they would need to do the opposite in the other. The silence was overbearing today, so Mike decided to take a chance at talking.

"You hear Coach come up on us?"

Mikell was a bit surprised to hear him speak, but as he too felt the weight of the silence, he decided to oblige. "Nah, he got them stealthy ninja skills."

Mike laughed silently. "Yeah, that guy failed straight outta ninja college. Got shipped here to coach basketball as a fallback. Hope his coaching is better than his ninja talents."

"His whistling be better than anything. I'm used to whistles by coaches, refs, and even the crowd, but that old man is on his own level. I'm learning to tune all his

105

whistling out. My brain catches those whistles and turns them into beats instead." - Mikell was curious why he was offering that much.

Mike considered this. He kind of liked the idea but felt funny admitting it to this kid he was determined to not like. In lieu of an actual answer, all he offered up was a: "Uh-huh."

The two continued their duties in silence that day, but from that point forward their interactions became less harsh. It was a tenuous bond they seemed to develop. Both were eager to dislike the other for past transgressions and the blame for the punitive measures being taken against them, but being angry at yet another person in his life was something Mike's mind couldn't handle, and Mikell's didn't want to bother handling.

***

Though the walk was a quiet one, they headed to Lancing's office. The door was locked and he did not seem to be inside. Confused about whether to call it a day or to wait for some unknown period of time, the two silently hung around the coach's door. Several minutes passed by when they heard a noise around the corner. They eagerly straightened up from their slouching positions against the wall and glanced towards the edge waiting for Lancing to come around the corner. However, it was just the janitor who showed up dragging the mop bucket behind him. Deflated, they went back against the wall, Mike pulling out his phone and scrolling through his Facebook feed.

As the janitor passed by them silently, he gave them a questionable look. Several feet later he stopped and turned halfway. "You waiting for the coach?"

"Yeah.."- Mikell replied.

"He at the gym, with some other coach folks. Must have forgotten you were coming by." - said the janitor, shrugged, and shuffled down the hallway rolling his mop bucket.

"Good of him to be clear about where we need to meet. Ready?" - asked Mike, putting his phone in his pocket.

Mikell nodded, and the duo headed down toward the gym, hoping that Lancing wouldn't somehow find his way back to his office by the time they got there. Neither had enough energy to run back and forth in a game of musical coach.

***

Mike and Mikell entered the gym, seeing Lancing writing something down in the corner while a couple of other coaches were packing up their things. When he heard them shuffling over, he turned slightly, glancing over his shoulder.

"'Bout damn time you two got here. Thought you forgot." - he sneered.

"We thought you were gonna be at...." - Mikell started.

"Work out your teammate chemistry in and work the crap you got going on out yet? Hope you purged all of your vile so you can concentrate on what you need to: winning basketball games" - Lancing interrupted.

"Well we ain't beating each other's asses...wait...teammates? We didn't even make the team yet, coach." - Mike shot back, confused.

Lancing turned around fully and got up. "You might be the dumbest smart kid I met in a while, Cassidy. Do you think we went through the efforts and pulled the strings on you two just so you wouldn't make the team? Come on...get real here, boys! You were on the team the moment you agreed to show up here."

"So what was all this punishment for? I had to lie to my Pops about practicing for the team, and I don't like lying to him. He knows when I lie, even if doesn't tell me!" - Mikell felt a bit heated now.

"Punishment? Well, if you want to look at it that way, but as your teammate here pointed out, you aren't beating each other's asses, right? So, your private practice session with one of your most talented teammates worked out for the best, didn't it? Did you feel punished to play the game we all love? Bet you two get along now much better than before, probably criticizing each other's weak points on the court constructively too. Shit, may all punishments you endure in your life be that beneficial." - He wasn't even hiding the smart-ass smirk on his face at this point.

"So this was all a head game? That's messed up shit coach..." - Mike started.

"Yeah.." - Mikell nodded.

"You hear that old saying about basketball being 20% physical and 80% mental? Well, consider this the training you got for the mental part. You can't play against another team while you view your teammates as your rivals. I won't bore you with the speech about how the stupid amount of talent between the two of you can help any team win if you harmonize your abilities. I will tell you that the only way two great players get better is to challenge each other and bring their strengths together while drowning out each other's weaknesses. Bird and Parish...take that for example." This resonated with Mike.

"Iron sharpens iron...."- Mike said largely to himself.

"I think we are a few centuries past sword jokes, Cassidy, but ....sure, whatever suits you. No judgment here." - Lancing quipped. "Show up for practice with the other kids. We will see who makes the cut tomorrow. Take a break from your custodial services tomorrow."

Mike and Mikell exchanged glances. Neither one was going to complain about this being their current situation now. Silently they both turned to leave.

"Hey, ah....one more thing boys," - Lancing called out to them. "The other guys assume, but don't know that you are getting on the team, so let's act accordingly when you happen to make the draft tomorrow. And uh, no pretentious about anyone who doesn't make it. We don't need any more delays."

***

Mike walked up the steps to his Southie home with some relief in his heart. No more having to dodge the team status subject, just had to finally focus on getting his shit together. He took a deep breath, glanced at his phone, and headed inside. He was surprised to find his father home, having a phone call. His presence was acknowledged in the manliest way his father knew how, a couple of stiff pats on the shoulder. Then his father continued to pace around the house as he always did while on calls.

No sign of his mother anywhere though. Mike headed to the fridge, starving for a bit now. He dug in and pulled out a Gatorade, and a stack of deli sliced Genoa salami, a family favorite. Shutting the fridge he reached up to the cupboard and yanked down a loaf of sliced wheat bread.

Setting the Gatorade on the counter, Mike quickly slapped a few salami slices between two slices of bread and set the very basic sandwich on the counter as well. He wrapped up the loaf and the salami stack, putting them back in their respective places. In this house, letting food go bad because it's left sitting out due to pure laziness, was bound to get you exiled from the family.

He snapped up his sandwich and drink, grabbed his backpack, and headed to his room. Remembering he had at least an hour of homework, Mike rolled his eyes and tossed his backpack on the back of his chair. He scarfed down the sandwich and drained three-quarters of the Gatorade bottle, setting it with the cap on next to his bed.

If he was looking for energy from the food he just put away, he wasn't getting it. He needed time to decompress his day before he was going to settle in for his homework. He sat on his bed and picked up the remote, flipping his TV on. He quickly navigated to his DVR and popped an episode of Law & Order. He recorded these almost obsessively. Something about the legal process fascinated him to no end. The episode was one he had seen before, but he threw himself back on the bed anyhow, laying his phone next to him.

He let his eyes rest for a moment. He opened them again as he heard a squeaking of a door, one he has become very familiar with since the door was a squeaker since he was a kid. The house was dark, and his mom's shadow hovered outside the room. Mike shook off his sleep. The screensaver on his TV was going, indicating that he had been asleep for some time. So much for homework...

"Mom?" - Mike asked the departing shadow in the doorway.

His mom hesitated, then reentered his room. "I'm sorry buddy, I didn't realize you clonked out. I just wanted to tell you that I visited Eric today."

Mike sat up. "How is he now?" The last time his parents attempted to visit Eric, he was going through serious withdrawals and unlike the devious zombie Eric he was used to, this one was just an outright maniacal asshole. His mother came home in tears from the things he said to her. Things that a son would never say to his mother. She knew it was the withdrawal demons speaking through him, and it was still her son in there, trapped behind a wall of poison, but it didn't make it hurt any less.

"He is actually better. He was certainly calmer, but I think he is taking a different approach. He realized the angry, violent outbursts wouldn't help, so he moved on to the next stage, pleading for that poison he has been putting in his body. He cries, and says he will die without the drugs. A rough thing for a mother to endure...."

"Mom....you know it's just the addiction talking. There was a time Eric was a great kid." - Mike reminded. He could hardly remember those times though.

"He was...and yes, of course I know it's the damned disease. That's why I am trying to brush it off my shoulders when he says the hideous things he says or when he begs as if his life depends on it. But listen, this is a step in the right direction, I really want to believe that. And you, I wanted to say how sorry I am." - Mom surprised Mike with that last one.

"What...mom you don't need to be....what even for??" - Mike stumbled all over his words.

"Barely been giving your life and your accomplishment any attention, it isn't fair. You are just as much my son, in some ways maybe more. So what is the verdict?" - she asked, forcing a smile.

What a relief to not have to hide it anymore and constantly prepare a fabricated representation of his status. "I made the team mom, practices are starting, and they are going to be intense. Coach is a.....well he is a whistler."

This prompted a burst of laughter from his mother, a sound and emotion that triggered a laugh from Mike as well. They laughed together. Mike realized this is the first time it had happened in years.

Chapter 13

Practices under Lancing were no joke. One would think the guy was training the Dream Team out there, as hard as he ran the boys around the gym. Mike took a while to get winded, but the practices were draining him. To make matters worse, their water breaks were half an hour apart out of two-hour practices, so by the time Lancing blew the water break whistle (just another in a series of ear-splitting whistling tirades he would go on), the boys were practically crawling to their bottles.

Mikell and Mike were selected for the team without too many questions as to why they made it over some others. Some kids trying out had heart but their skill level was so far lacking, Lancing and the other coaches could not bring themselves to put these kids on the team, if not to save the team's face, but the boys themselves. About 22 kids tried out, 12 made the cut, and much like a federal jury the coaches picked three alternates. One of the alternates ended up being Asher, and he was not happy about it at all, relegated to ride the bench for yet another season.

Unfortunately for Mikell, Asher's racially questionable ethics made it so that his blame for not making the team squared directly on his new Dorchester teammate. Asher would turn beat-red and grit his teeth every time Mikell was in his line of sight, mumbling racial profanities under his breath. What drove him more crazy is that Mike and Mikell seemed to be civil, and he was out the one partner he thought he had in disliking this Dorchester misfit.

Mikell felt the vibes, he was used to this feeling from the general Boston public when he ventured outside of his predominantly black Dorchester neighborhood. He had learned to relegate it to the back of his mind long ago, and move on with his life, taking the 'mind over matter' approach: if he didn't mind, the haters didn't matter. Asher was not going to suddenly change his perspective, so there was no reason to try to do anything about it or let it bother him. This was just the way of the world. Pops taught him that lesson long ago.

Mike felt Asher's vibes too. He was in a predicament between not screwing up his team, his future at the school, avoiding making things even harder for his parents, who had enough to deal with Eric's constant array of mishaps, and alienating Asher, the kid who was one of the first and only friends he made at the school so far. His solution was to just stay out of the situation. This was made harder when Asher tried to vent his frustrations to him. Now it was even more awkward for Mike. He had to both have Asher believe that he sympathized with his frustrations without ever saying anything that would indicate to anyone else that he actually agreed.

Truthfully, he was realizing that he lived in the company of many people who were quite ignorant when it came to those from backgrounds that differed. He felt a sense of shame for at one time actually thinking that the nonsense people tended to believe was actually factual. Perhaps his time with Mikell as a teammate opened his eyes a bit. He was no longer that prick from Dorchester, he was a hell of a ballplayer, and not a bad guy overall. Mike still felt that he shouldn't like him, so he convinced himself of reasons to believe that was the case. It struck Mike as odd that in many ways Mikell's personality was similar to his own, he already realized their taste in music aligned, they both were clearly passionate about basketball, and they had one other thing in common: they seemed to be the only two who never made reference or said anything about their families.

Mike had his reasons. His family's struggles were private and no one's business, especially considering the crazy shit going on at his house currently. He couldn't help but wonder if Mikell was holding on to something similar. It was easy to think that he lived a rough life in the Dorchester hoods, but he was around people that have known him since he was a kid, so he must have had friends, former teammates, parents, etc. What he didn't have here is a friend. Asher was an ignorant turd, Mike would readily admit, but he reached out to a new kid when no one else did. Mike always wondered if that was because Asher didn't have much along the way of real friends himself.

But Mikell was different. He was fine with the team, communicative when he needed to be, attentive when others were speaking, and even chill about Lancing's loud coaching style. He did keep to himself though, pretty much anytime he was not on the court. Mike would see him between classes in the halls and on breaks. He would always be alone. In a way, he was more of a misfit than the one Mike felt like.

***

Mike did make another friend, Lucia, a brunette whose cuteness and smile made Mike feel uneasy in the best way possible. They sat next to each other in two classes and several seats apart in another three. Mike caught Lucia looking around and smiling at him, and she would come over and talk to him any chance she got. She was nowhere near a pestering weirdo though. She had a wit as sharp as her tongue, and when he made her laugh, she would touch his chest or shoulders casually. Mike tried to resist the thought that Lucia was into him. In his eyes, a girl that was chill and good-looking was far out of his league. He tried to observe her interactions with other guys she talked to, not in a creepy stalker way, but more as a casual observation.

Her mannerisms were similar, but there was a lot less touching and way less eye contact.

Mike wrestled with whether he should act on the vibe he was getting from Lucia, it certainly felt like she wanted his attention. If he waited too long, and she was into him, she would think he didn't want to reciprocate. If he did and she was just being friendly, there would be some serious awkwardness. His hormones pushed him to it, but his head made him doubt himself, for no less the reason that if things went off the rails with her, or even if they didn't, his mind would need to splinter off in yet another direction. He was already struggling with keeping it right between things at home, schoolwork, and basketball. How would introducing a girl into the equation going to fare?

Mike thought about Lucia and making a move for a week, and would finally decide that he had nothing to lose if he played it cool. One of the driving factors was that family stuff seemed to be calming down a bit. Eric had actually stayed at a rehab facility for over 10 days, though he did attempt to run away once and had to be restrained and locked in a room. His mom went to visit Eric several times. Even his father did, but Mike did not. However, based on what he heard from his parents, Eric was in a better place. He was quiet, likely resigned to the fact that he was being forced from his addiction, and perhaps feeling guilty and regretful of the things he had done.

By the end of the second week of being on the team, Mike felt he was in a decent place mentally, so he decided he would take a chance on asking Lucia to hang out. In the back of his mind, he knew most people in his life would be uneasy with him dating a Hispanic girl, at best, and combative to the idea at worst. Some part of him wondered if it would be worth it to him, there were other girls out there, on the other hand, he learned something vital from being around Mikell. He definitely put up with a lot of shit from ignorant people, and he brushed it off, at least visually not letting it affect his life. Was he a lesser man than Mikell then?? Letting what others think to dictate his life decisions in pursuing his happiness. No way! Mike was not going to be one of those.

He worked up the nerve to ask Lucia to hang out. But he needed a place to take her. Too private might creep her out, too public and it would be too "friend-like"...not his exact intent. As he scrolled through his phone walking home at the end of the week, an ad for a local show popped up on his Facebook feed. Brooklyn-based drill rapper Sleepy Hollow was playing at the Paradise Rock Club in Boston next weekend. He doubted Lucia enjoyed that scene, she certainly didn't seem the type, but he had learned to not assume "types" recently. The tickets were cheap enough, and he was working his ass off. He had some gift cards gathering dust in his room, so this was the perfect chance to use them up. Worst comes to worst, Lucia would want to bail, and it gives them a reason for a more private hangout.

Mike waited for her outside her class on Monday, risking running late to practice, and asked if she wanted to watch the practice. He angled it as "wanna see how much whistling coach really does?" It was a running joke he had put forward to her before. He rolled the dice on her taking him up on it, but to his surprise, she was more than happy to do so. On their way to the gym, he asked her what type of music she listened to, and Lucia surprised him by professing her love for hard rock and metal but was quick to follow up with being open to every music genre under the sun. Cute, witty, and open-minded...why the hell is this girl seems so into him then, Mike wondered.

Once she opened the door, Mike walked through it, asking if she would be into checking out a rap show in Boston with him. From her reaction, it was obvious to Mike that this is what she was hoping he would ask her for. The concert idea was a perfect, public place, but they'd be there together, like private and public at the same time. They worked out a plan to meet up at a T-stop, and hop on the green line, to hit up the show the following Saturday. Lucia then hung around for a few minutes of practice, until Lancing started to notice a random girl watching the game from the sidelines. She signaled to Mike that she had to go, and he nodded in agreement.

Asher picked up on this too and attempted to start conversations with Mike about it. Mike didn't really want Asher fucking this up for him, so he kept the situation mostly tightlipped, responding with only casual responses, very light on details. During practice, Lancing insisted on a scrimmage, where Mike began to realize the thing he feared would happen was going to happen: he began to have distraction lapses. Strangely, hardship at home seemed to give him a reason to not think about the home situation and focus on the goings-on on the court, but being excited about hanging out with Lucia, actually diverted his focus away. He had to regain his composure. Lack of focus, in the face of any other thoughts or stressors on his mind, was something he could simply not permit. The real recognition came when Mikell drove around him for an easy layup, and on the next possession, stuffed a shot out of his hands. Shaking anything else off his mind, Mike refocused his mind on practice.

This wasn't the time to screw around. The season and the first game was coming up on Friday, after all.

***

Mikell was lost in thought as he shuffled up to his Dorchester home, wrapping up a tiring practice, and a

122

long school week, blasting beats in his years, staring out into the street, yet reacting to traffic and other pedestrians around him purely out of instinct, much in the same way that someone driving along a highway when they are tired, for miles and miles on end, suddenly realizing that they don't recognize how far they have gone or where they are, but they are there safely.

It was in this daze that Mikell nearly ran into Isaiah, a childhood friend, one of his oldest, and stopped short as his friend stepped out in front of him, startling him into a sudden stop. Mikell took a second to get his bearings but seeing Isaiah's face couldn't help but smile, pull down his headphones and embrace his long-time friend.

"Whatcha doin' here man?" - he quickly asked.

"Bearing gifts for my less than an attentive brother. How you been? Haven't seen your ass around school, thought you gone and dropped out, then remembered your dad would roast your ass before he ever allowed that." - Isaiah shot back sarcastically. "Then I heard you switched up schools on us. Didn't tell nobody, you get in shit with the law or somethin'?"

Considering his family's past, this was a sensitive button to push, but Mikell had to forgive. He wasn't exactly forthcoming about why he suddenly left Dorchester and didn't tell anyone. "Nah, got recruited

123

to play ball at a different school. More promise there for me and Pops than where things were going before. How you been? Did you say something about gifts? I'd body a man for some nachos right now." - Mikell smirked, then looked around to make sure the dark humor was discreet enough.

"Easy son, no need for that today. I got no nachos for you anyway, but I got something better." - Isaiah pulled out his phone and start tapping in his login.

"Ain't nothin better than some nachos right now, man, everything else is inferior." - Mikell joked.

"You're thinking small. I got some shit for us to dig into, and a chance for you to stamp yourself hard and get some respect on your name and your talents." - Isaiah kept scrolling through something on his phone. "I ain't cappin', this shit is real, and if you do this, you could change life for you and your Pops"

Now Mikell was getting half curious, half concerned. Isaiah was not one to bullshit him around, and he was not one to throw around ideas he couldn't follow up on, but he did have a tendency of mixing with seedy assholes if he thought there was some benefit to him out of it.

"Ah...here!" - Isaiah raised his phone and turned it to Mikell. Mikell looked close at the small print and a barcode underneath. Leaning in he realized that he was looking at what looked like an ad for a rap show at the Paradise Rock Club. Isiah's thumb was covering half the artist's name but the first part read "Sleepy" Mikell dug in his brain a moment, and then it clicked. Sleepy Hollow was playing at the PRC, and he was staring at what looked like a ticket.

"Sleepy Hollow? He has some good shit. When you going?" - Mikell asked. Isaiah stared at him with sarcastic eyeballs. Mikell backed his face up staring back.

"So yo ass thinks I came all the way over here to say I bring gifts, just to show you a ticket for me to go see Sleepy Hollow? You think I got nothin' better to do in my life? No, dumbass, I am not going, we are going! A week from tomorrow, so don't make plans." - Isaiah shot back grinning at the tail end.

"Man...that would be the show for the year but come on, you know I don't got the money for a ticket, and I am not asking Pops for a loaner." - Mikell answered. He was a big fan of Sleepy Hollow and this would definitely be a show to see.

"You need to transfer back to Dorchester, that new school of yours has made you a dense fucking dumbass, son! You forget how gifts work, now??" - Isaiah came back. "You ever know a gift you had to pay for? I got the damn tickets right here in front of your face, you comin' with me. But I got more...my cousin, you remember Curt? Well, he lived out in Brooklyn for a minute and got friendly with this up-and-coming drill rapper out there. You connected the dots yet?"

Mikell was making the connection and this was getting him psyched up more. "So Curt knows Sleepy?"

"Yeah Einstein, he knows him. Well enough to get us backstage to hang with him before the show. And Sleepy got connections to producers and other people of importance for those who got a knack for the beats and words. You hearin' me?" - Isaiah was grinning now.

Mikell was taken aback. Isaiah knew he was a diehard rap fan, and he was one of the few people that knew Mikell's knack for writing and hammering out beats. He had a lot going on, and he knew nothing would come of this, but the ticket was there for him, and he had a chance to meet Sleepy Hollow. How the hell would he turn this down?

"My first game of the season is on Friday, but Saturday...I mean shit, I don't pass up on gifts, especially not ones like that!" - Mikell smiled and raised his hand to Isaiah who grabbed it, as the two pulled in and bumped elbows.

"There you go, bring your A-game, and I don't just mean to the court on Friday. Bring a good attitude and a clear dome to the show. I'll text you when we catching the train out there. Now I got other people to see and make smile, but these would be females, so I'm out, but yeah, kick some ass and bring that fire I know you got." - Isaiah put his phone away and tapped Mikell on the back. Then he raced down the street.

Mikell took a breath. That was unexpected and yet, he realized he was still smiling.

Chapter 14

It was game day. The team psyched themselves up from the locker room but walked out onto the court hesitantly. The debut of the newly revamped team of World Leadership Prep did not escape the attention of the hardcore high school basketball fanbase in Boston, especially with the news that two central figures from the BNBL conflict a couple of years back were somehow teammates now on this very squad.

The crowd that filed into the newly cleaned-up gym was impressive. Mikell looked around to see many faces, not of his skin color, which gave him mixed feelings. On the one hand, less of a chance that someone from Dorchester would be there to see a potential failure from the team, but on the other, it was an isolating feeling. He didn't want to assume he was surrounded by a crowd that would be viscerally hostile to him, but it is a feeling he could not shake.

The overwhelming number of white faces did however have one particular advantage. He was able to spot anyone of different skin color from the sea of faces easily, specifically Pops. Travis walked in and found a seat, scanning the court for his son. He then quietly raised his hand. Mikell nodded back to him to show that Travis was noticed.

***

Mike tried really hard to push his excitement about the concert tomorrow, and more importantly his date with Lucia out of his mind for the sake of the game, but it just wasn't happening. He tried to run through the practiced plays for what felt like the 300th time in his head, but his mind always drifted back. He tried to distance himself from those thoughts by looking around the gym. He knew that neither of his parents would be able to make it with everything going on at home, his mom interviewing for jobs, and his father busy with the latest construction project. That burned him a bit, but he assured himself that they would be there for future games. Unless he got so distracted that he stunk up the place and got himself booted from the team.

He looked over to Mikell who, quietly, as usual, was putting up jumpers and interchanging them with layups. Lancing was busy talking to the assistant coaches on the sidelines as they would point to spots on the court. Perhaps they were planning the things they'd need to work on when World Leadership Prep got smoked in their first game. It's that thought that shook him free of his distraction trance. For the next hour and change, he would need to go into pure basketball mode, and nothing else should matter.

He focused on landing his practice shots. At one point, the ball recoiled against a shot Asher put up and was sent flying off to the side. Mike darted a glance at Asher who shrugged and continued his shootaround, then took off chasing after the ball which was quickly bouncing toward the crowd. A guy in the front of the stands caught it and looked at Mike sharply.

"Don't embarrass us, kid!" - he said, handing Mike the ball back.

Mike turned around before gritting his teeth. He felt the fan pressure before, so he could shake it off. He had played at a level higher than this and had long since stopped being rattled by fan commentary. One could not concentrate on the game if they listened to hecklers and cheers too much. What caught Mike's attention and instantly made him forget his interaction is Lucia in the front row on the opposite side of the court from where he was now standing. She didn't see him looking and was busy talking to her friend, but it made Mike's gritted teeth turn into a grin of relief. But now he really couldn't embarrass himself, or the team. That would not be a good note to send this potential....whatever this would be after tomorrow, in the right direction.

As he hung his eyes on Lucia, he was jolted by a whistle and realized that he must have been standing and staring at her for well over a minute which made him feel awkward as hell. He put up one more jumper, chased down the ball, and headed back to the sidelines.

World Leadership Prep was playing one of their historically deep rivals in the Mass Tech Prep, a school for those kids inclined to attach themselves to math, science, and technology, and went lighter on the liberal arts. But they supposedly had a good basketball system, or so it was advertised from their perspective.

The team's players seemed undersized, but Mikell knew better than to underestimate that. His height and skill gave him a great advantage on the court, but in basketball, speed was a killer. He had been on the losing end of quite a few games where the team simply had circles run around them by faster, shorter players who basically had a field day with open shots because they were damn near impossible to catch.

Seeing the team warming up became a bit concerning. The Tech's passing game seemed solid, and one could tell this team had played together for at least a season, while World Leadership Prep was throwing together a bunch of elements. But as many teams in the NBA had proven again and again, a group of stars does not a team make. Concerns about getting outplayed started to creep around in Mikell's mind, but he forced himself to shake them off. Lancing did say this game was a lot more mental than physical, and he refused to get beaten before the game started.

From tip-off on, it was clear that Mikell's concerns were warranted. The players on the opposing team were ridiculously fast and were unapologetically showing off their passing game. Behind the back, through the legs of World Leadership Prep players, and fakeouts on every other possession. Mikell decided that he can only do what he can do to contribute to his team, but he should not have to shoulder the entire load.

Strangely, he didn't touch the ball for the first four possessions, a fact that only occurred to him when he finally received a pass. He was well-positioned near the rim, which allowed him to put up an easy layup. Once he scored, the crowd cheered. Mikell wondered why it felt so unexpected and out of place. Perhaps he was used to his home crowd.

***

The game was fast-paced and with only a few stops. There was surprisingly little in terms of penalties, which was a weird feeling after practicing under Coach Lancing, the whistle-machine. Mike was able to maneuver himself nicely on the defensive end, being able to make three steals in the first quarter, converting them into points on two breakaways. Both were met with loud pops from the crowd, who was eating things up. But the game was far from a walk in the park. As the first quarter neared the end, Tech switched to zone defense, and Mike foolishly got caught surrounded by three defenders, with his heel nearly on the sideline. His only out was to pass.

The problem was that he was falling backward, and the defenders had their hands in his eyes, obstructing any view of nearby passers. Then from the corner of his eye, he saw a friendly jersey, only to quickly realize it was the least friendly jersey among the crew, Mikell. But there was no way out of this one, so he chucked the ball over and went down as the momentum landed him on his ass out of bounds.

The defenders turned quickly only to watch Mikell sidestep the team's center and leap up to roll the ball into the hoop. Mike didn't know whether to be excited or embarrassed, but the time it took him to figure that out was spent with a roar from the crowd and the Tech team racing down the court while he was still sitting down.

Snapping back to reality, Mike quickly pushed himself from the ground but by this point, he was the last player left on that half of the court. The point guard of the Tech team swung the ball over in a dangerous manner, cutting across a third of the court to a wide-open small forward who nailed a long jumper right from behind the arc, right as the buzzer went off. The same small forward whose job on the court it was for Mike to guard. He glanced in Lancing's direction. He caught the end of a frustrated glare. Then Lancing called everyone else to the huddle.

***

Toward the end of the first half, Mikell got himself 2 blocks and 11 points, as well as a very awkward assist. During a timeout, he was surprised to catch an earful from Lancing for playing silently on the court instead of communicating with the team. "They are good ballplayers, but they haven't mastered mind reading yet, have you?" - Lancing asked him with scathing sarcasm. Mikell resolved to change that in the second half.

After a halftime period that seemed like it was over in 3 minutes, Mikell was instructed to ride the bench. This surprised him since he started the game, but Lancing hinted at this being necessary in order to make sure that he wasn't winded for later in the game. The scoreboard had WLP up by 9, but this was not indicative of how the game was going. They were not on their best-playing terms and the entire team knew it. Players tended to blame their teammates externally, but internally they criticized themselves. Mikell certainly did the latter.

Mikell watched Mike start the second half and have a pretty decent showing. Seemed like falling on his ass earlier in the game, then faltering on his guarding duties paid off in the fact that his humiliation drove him to play harder. He was dishing out assists and putting up spot-up jumpers. With less than 4 minutes left in the third, Mike had himself a healthy 19 points and 5 assists, as well as 4 steals for the game.

With under 3 minutes to go, Lancing suddenly motioned for Mikell to get in the game. Mikell headed to the check-in table, as Lancing yelled to him that he was coming in for Mike. This caught Mikell by surprise. What is the coach doing here? Playing his two best players around each other? What was the point of having them go up against each other?

His confusion was soon thwarted by a sudden scoring onslaught brought on by the opposing team, who stole the ball twice, nailed a three, a layup, and added a free throw to boot. By the end of the third quarter, Tech pulled within 3 points. The buzzer could not have gone off soon enough. The momentum they had was carrying them right to the lead.

During the last quarter break, Lancing huddled the team together and laid out a strategy that would focus on prioritizing defense, a point he offered preached during practices. Then he instructed Mike, Mikell, and three other boys to head out to the court. Mike played for most of the third quarter, and while he ripped it up, he was visibly winded. How is this helping anyone, Mikell wondered.

***

Mike would have killed for a 2-minute breather, but he was running hot on his offense, though admittedly subpar on the defensive end. Hearing that Lancing was putting him right back into the game was a bit surprising, but he was happy to get the minutes, especially with Lucia watching. There he goes again, thinking about showing up for the girl, when he should be showing up for his family, for his new team, for his coach, and for his future.

Mike shook the thought from his brain and headed back onto the court. The whistle blew and Tech inbounded the ball into the game. Mike was guarding the player to who the ball was passed, so he attempted to yank another steal out of the deal. Unfortunately, he was a bit too far from the pass, and it swept just outside of his reach. He tried to stop short to turn around, but at that point, he left the player with the ball open, heading straight for the rim. As he went up for what would have been a sure thing of a layup, Mikell came out of nowhere to swat the ball out of his hands.

Mike was not going to be shown up like this. He pivoted back to the court as the ball went out of bounds. Chad Feeny, the point guard, inbounded the ball right to Mike who dribbled it up the court. Seeing an opening, he shifted the ball back to Feeny and cut to the basket. Mikell came from the other end. Feeny darted the ball to Mike, but it was a little late, Mike had already had his momentum carry him right past the hoop. Mikell had just passed him, crossing towards the rim. Mike allowed his instinct to take over and scooped the ball right to Mikell who rose to the rim landing a floater. The play was like something straight out of a highlight reel, and the crowd responded in kind.

It just dawned on Mike what had happened. Mikell glanced at him as they backpedaled up the court, and Mike gave him a shrug indicating indifference, as Mikell rolled his eyes with a half-hearted grin. This may have been the first time Mike saw anything that looked like a smile on Mikell's face.

***

The fourth quarter continued in a surprisingly lackluster fashion. While motivated by the hype of the big play, the inability to stand the idea of the other looking good on the court, somewhat suppressed Mike and Mikell's drive. Lancing noticed and he was not happy. They could tell by the fact that he turned red-faced every time they passed up on a shot or a pass to each other, which they entirely avoided for the rest of the game. Both seemed to want to lead the team to victory, but neither was willing to share the honor with their nemesis. The lack of comradery showed as they allowed Mass-Tech to get right back into the game, and even overtake the lead due to a series of foolish and unnecessary fouls.

It was only by the Patesh's ridiculous three-point accuracy that their team got back to a two-point lead with 35 seconds remaining in the game. Patesh was also fouled on the three-pointer. He nailed the shot but missed the free throw which was rebounded by the center from Mass Tech. The tall boy cleared the swarming defenders around him with swinging elbows, then passed the ball to the team's point guard who took his time bringing the ball up the court. With just over 15 seconds on the clock, the point guard shot the ball over to the corner, where the small forward drained a jumper, tying the game.

Lancing was beside himself. He called a timeout and laid out a play that required Mike and Mikell to work together. Neither one was interested in the least, but they were not going to sacrifice the game out of spite. It was simply not in their competitive nature. They headed out to the court where Patesh inbounded the ball to Feeny, who passed it out to the three-point arc to Mike. Mike faked a shot sending the defender flying at him through the air. But as soon as he took off the ground, Mike darted around him toward the basket. The center stepped in his path.

As Lancing drew it up, the play was going exactly as planned, with Mikell coming up behind the center. Mike tossed the ball around the defender's hips, landing the ball in Mikell's hands. Mikell, with no one blocking him, adjusted and went up for a short jumper, but in an unanticipated occurrence, the power forward from Mass Tech slapped the ball from behind with 3 and half seconds on the clock left to go.

The hand connected with the ball which was already being propelled in a particular direction. The ball traveled on its intended path, but with way more power than Mikell intended, causing it to bounce off the back of the rim. The hand got more than just the ball though, nailing Mikell's wrist in the process.

The whistle blew immediately to stop play, having just under 3 seconds remaining on the clock and sending Mikell to the line. Breathing heavy and rubbing his wrist, Mikell went to the line and the ref bounced the ball to him for a free throw. Mikell remembered the criticism of buckling under the pressure, and he focused extremely hard on the rim and his form. The ball went up, bouncing on the back of the rim, then on its side, and then falling through the net. Mikell breathed a sigh of relief. He looked over at Travis in the stands. Pops was standing up staring intently. Mikell got the ball again, spun it in his hands, bounced it once, and was set to put it up when the whistle blew stopping his progress and breaking his concentration. Totally by design, the Mass Tech coach called a time-out.

***

"Rebound, rebound, rebound, and rebound!" - Lancing repeated to the squad. "If the shot misses, we need to get the ball and either burn the clock or take a foul again, they're over the limit, so we will be at the stripe again."

Mikell headed back to the line, with the "rebound" idea in his head. Lancing may have done the opposite of what he actually hoped for here. Mikell felt unsure but had to try. He put up the shot, and it bounced off the side of the rim landing directly into the hands of the shooting guard from the opposing squad. The Mass Tech coach then called their final timeout. Mikell was pissed, Lancing insisting on rebounding psyched him out and he knew it, but it's something he'd never admit.

He zoned out Lancing's hot-headed diatribe that followed his screw-up and looked around to see his Pops. Pops was sitting down, elbows on his knees, staring at the court intently. The whistle blew and the players headed back to the court. Mass-Tech inbounded and with only a second and change to go, the point guard went to put up a jumper. Mikell only had a chance to turn to see Mike Cassidy flying at the shooter, hand in his face. The buzzer went off as the ball clunked off the backboard and fell away, giving WLP a 1 point win.

The crowd went nuts. Their team won, but Mikell knew this was a victory they backed into. He headed back to the bench and picked up a towel. Before heading to greet the opposing team midcourt, he heard Lancing say: "Cassidy, Sharp, see me after the post-game meeting." Winded and tired, Mikell threw the towel over his head. As he looked up, he caught an obnoxiously devious smirk on Asher's face. He headed to mid-court. He was glad for the win but completely unproud of how it transpired.

This weekend should help him forget about things....at least for a while.

Chapter 15

The T train rattled swiftly back and forth as Mikell subtly bounced along in tandem to the beat in his earbuds that seemed to go right along with the beat somehow. On the playlist, Sleepy Hollow was dropping lines, the only thing to listen to when heading to the concert after all. Mikell felt a little annoyed at hearing the train rumble through his earbuds. Noise-canceling headphones had really spoiled him, but he wasn't bringing those to the show. Too many stories of people getting patted down, and anything besides phones, keys, and wallets was made to be put in a "holding" bin or tossed. The "holding" bin only held the damn things until someone who was not the owner decided to lift them. No need to risk his quality headphones there.

His thoughts drifted to yesterday's game and the team squeaking out a win. He loved the suspense of close games when he watched basketball, but he was more than happy with a blowout when he was on the court. His adrenaline would pump the same without the unease and anxiety.

Mikell checked the time on his phone. He was supposed to be meeting Isaiah early. Sounds like he was going to meet Sleepy Hollow today. He didn't even know what to expect or what he would say, but he wouldn't pass up on the opportunity. Sleepy Hollow wasn't a giant star by any means, but he was a quality up-and-coming drill rapper that Isaiah thought Mikell should meet. Apparently, Isaiah had some grand notions of how good Mikell was at the rap game. Mikell saw himself as just ok. But if there was a connection to be made here, why not, he figured.

He glanced around the train car, packed with people, and thought the space around him was fairly clear. That's why he liked sitting on the far ends of train cars in the T, no matter the line. Most passengers were always hesitant about missing their stops. Some were new to the area, didn't know where they were going very well, and needed to be paranoid about being close to the door at all times. Others simply got anxious when thinking about having to push their way through the crowd. He would often see people sitting across the car from the side of the train where the doors opened to the platform get up and move to the door two stops ahead of time just to not somehow be stuck. I guess they had places to be pretty urgently.

Mikell put his head down and looked at the floor as the next track started. He closed his eyes and bobbed his head to the beat a bit. Tonight was going to be fun as hell, just had to get through it without some bad luck following him around. Getting into the show for free and meeting Sleepy Hollow through Isaiah? Things were going a little too well. As his life's own personal rule of threes, for every two good things, some shit followed after. It really never failed. Then again, he figured he was used to it.

***

Mike met up with Lucia at the parking lot of the T stop. Mike got to the meeting stop first and was standing around fumbling on his phone. That's when Asher's texts started showing up. He wanted to know what Mike was up to and if he wanted to hang out. Mike was going to ignore his texts, but he had to do something with his time, so he tried a gentle brush off from the conversation, leaving out any details. Asher pressed him, and Mike finally got tired of playing the hiding game, after all, who cares right? So he told Asher he was going to a rap show with a friend. There was a long pause in the non-stop round of texting.

Mike saw the dots appear on his screen several times, showing that Asher was typing, but then nothing came through. Over 7 minutes later a short "wtf kid? You into that rap shit?" followed by. "Don't tell me you think that garbage is music." Mike rolled his eyes. He couldn't tell if Asher was being sarcastic, but he suspected that he wasn't. Before he could get a line typed out, more texts followed. "I mean if you're going for a bitty who is into that shit to get on up in there, you gotta endure some punishment for that I guess."

Mike erased his text. Timely move, Lucia was walking toward him at that very moment. She wasn't dolled out but she changed her look up enough that beyond the gorgeous dark eyes and face-melting smile, she had somehow got even more attractive in his eyes.

He quickly muted the phone and stood straight up, greeting her with a smile. She hugged him and put her head deep into his shoulder, then pulled away with a smile still on her face, and said: "Ready?" He nodded and they headed to the train.

South Station is a busy place on a typical afternoon, but on Saturday nights it's practically an overcrowded club bursting like an overtight sardine can. They walked into a busy, loud place, and it didn't take long for them to start to lose track of each other. Lucia, thinking quickly, grabbed a hold of Mike's hand. It startled him a bit, but a wave of relief washed over him immediately.

Their timing was perfect, the next train was just pulling in and they hopped on it, cramming among a crowd of people so tight that their bodies were pressed together. Mike didn't mind at all, and based on Lucia's facial expression, neither did she. A group of young men standing next to Lucia was screwing around with each other, acting as if they were on an open beach somewhere rather than a cramped train car. Mike would have had him and Lucia move away, but there really was nowhere to go, they were stuck mid-car, with these idiots next to them. It would be a long few stops unless these jokers got off the train.

***

Mikell excused his way through a crowd of people and hopped off at South Station. Checking the time, he raced down to the next platform just as a train was pulling away. Kicking himself for not moving faster, he sat on a bench. The stop was relatively empty seeing as that most people on it just hopped on the last train. He figured this was for the best. The next train would be less crammed.

To his surprise, the next train showed up rather quickly after the last one left. He took that to mean that the previous must have been running late. Mikell got up and got ready to get on, realizing he was one of two people on the platform. Simply not enough time had passed since the last train left for the platform to get full, even on this early Saturday night. Well, less crowd for him to deal with. Maybe he will even get a seat at the end of the car as he preferred.

He stepped up to the platform and stretched his arms over his head. The train was visible now. It entered the station but showed no signs of slowing down. The thing was absolutely packed, and to Mikell's surprise, blasted right through the station, never bothering to stop.

"What the fuck...?" - Mikell threw his hands up, then slapped them down by his sides. "Not enough people at the stop for ya?" This was not ideal. The ride and walk would take another 20 minutes, and he was supposed to meet Isaiah in 25. Cutting it close. He regretted not leaving earlier. He went and sat back down, noticing that more people were arriving at the station now.

The wait for the next train to come by felt like an eternity, or if Mikell's phone was to be believed nearly 10 minutes. When the train was finally audible from the tunnel, Mikell got up, realizing that the platform was swarming with people by this point. He was right about that two great things, one shitshow, now he was sure of it. It was entirely his streak all over again.

He edged as close as he could to the front. This time the train pulled in and stopped. The door in front of Mikell was right at the head of the car. He squeezed his way over to the previous car's doors and was able to sneak in. He even maneuvered himself off the steps that lead into the car and wrapped his arm around the pole. He pulled his phone out to check the time again. 15 minutes left. The train did not move. This was typical of South Station trains, waiting for more passengers. He didn't understand that now though, there was just way too many people, not like the train could even hold anymore.

The doors finally closed and the train lurched forward. Mikell dug around in his phone for some more music, trying to zone out. But not too much. The last thing he needed now was to miss his stop.

***

The train left the underground tunnel part of the line a couple of stops later, and as soon as it came above ground, he heard several sequential dings in Lucia's purse. She smiled an "eeeek" type of smile and said: "Sorry...I gotta... it's my mom, she....worries."

"I would too when you're out with shady characters like myself." - Mike joked.

Lucia laughed and dug in her purse for her phone, struggling to pull it free within a cramped space. She finally got the phone out and swiped it open. Mike looked around the train hearing the loud voices of the kids next to them. They were still rowdy, clearly not aware of their immediate surroundings.

Mike kept looking around for a chance to move them somewhere, anywhere else but away from these idiots, but there was hardly room to lift an elbow, never mind to move over. Lucia was busy trying to type a text to her mom while keeping her balance. As Mike had feared, the tallest of the knuckleheads behind Lucia decided it would be a great idea to take the drink his friend was holding away from him and lifted it in the air, just shy of his friend's reach. The other idiot started jumping in the air to try to get it. There is no way this was going to end well.

Lucia finished up her text and had just put her phone back in her purse, when the second idiot jumped up and reached for the drink, grabbing it. The first idiot was still holding on to it, resulting in both of them squeezing the bottom, which made the lid pop off, and the contents sprayed up into the air landing down Lucia's back and the bottom of her hair. She was wearing her jacket but there was enough liquid to soak it right through. She was stunned and shivered from the cold.

The first idiot, who got the brunt of the spillage shook off the surprise and threw the now nearly empty cup at his friend's chest. "The fuck...you got me soaked, son? Chill!" The second idiot didn't answer he was looking at Lucia who was miserably trying to shake off the unexpected cold and wet sensation. He stared for another moment and then burst out laughing. The first idiot turned to see what was funny, as did their two friends and they all burst out laughing.

Mike shook off his own stunned demenour and acted on instinct, turning Lucia around and switching places with her to distance her, even if it was another 2 feet further from this band of jackals. Other people around them began to protest, but they were all mid-ride, stuck with these buffoons. Mike didn't say much at first, just gritted his teeth, but seeing Lucia's radiant smile gone from her face, he couldn't help himself.

"Laugh it up, shitheads! Good thing you are the only people riding the T. Wouldn't want to ruin someone's day. Assholes!" - He snapped with biting sarcasm.

The pack of jackals stood silent for a minute, silencing their laughter except for idiot number two who continued to snicker so hard he started snorting. Then idiot number one saw his chance to turn this into a provocation.

"Why you worried? Just made your little hooker wet for you. You weren't gonna do it!"

Mike felt the blood in his veins boiling. He had to say something back but the words were eaten up by his anger. Lucia was trying to wriggle out of her wet jacket. Mike realized that he was wearing the jacket that Lancing had gifted the team's players when he formally picked them for the team. Mike quickly started getting out of his own jacket, and once he was out, helped Lucia with hers. Then he put his over her and took her jacket folding it over his arm without saying a word.

"Oh shit, of the two of them, I think it's him that's the wet pussy!" - said one of the idiots' friends.

An older gentleman from their other side tried to intervene, but the idiots brushed him off like he was nothing. Mike couldn't look Lucia in the eye if he didn't do something to stand up for her.

***

Mikell was lost in the music when the crowd around him suddenly nailed him like a tidal wave. He had to grab tightly to the bar next to him in order to keep from falling backward on the nervous elderly lady standing behind him with a little girl who was presumably her granddaughter. He nearly dropped his phone, so he instinctually grasped it tighter. He then looked up to see what was going on. About fifteen feet ahead there must have been a fight happening. The crowd around was pushed the other way like the middle was parting into some kind of human sinkhole. There were women's screams that pierced his ears even with the music blasting through his buds.

Mikell pulled the earbuds loose and tucked his phone away, looking up over the crowd trying to figure out what was going on. Looked like a shoving match, and a fight going on. Mikell saw a young woman pushed back and what looked like 4 kids jumping someone right in the middle of a moving train car. People were getting on their phones to try to call the cops. A young guy in a suit tried to intervene and got punched in the face.

Mikell was sure this was not his scene to get involved in but after hearing a girl screaming for the band of kids to stop repeatedly and seeing the terrified people's faces he decided he would do what he could. He tucked his phone away and slicked his way past the two people in front of him. He edged closer to the fight as the train pulled into the next stop. The doors opened and many people filed out of the train. He suspected this wasn't even their stop. Now the train was a little more open and he could see more of what was going on. He thought he recognized the girl, wearing what looked a lot like the same jacket he just got handed a week before by Lancing.

On the floor of the car was a kid getting the living shit beaten out of him by what looked like 3 thugs, and one more was standing behind them cheering them on. Mikell didn't know who was right or wrong here, but this was just fucked up. He remembered his brother, and how he would come home with bruises from gang initiations, though Mikell was far too young to understand what that meant at the time. It triggered something inside of him, so he got closer to the fight.

***

There was not a part of Mike's body that didn't hurt. He was pretty sure his nose was broken because he was bleeding everywhere. He forced his way up to his feet while getting kicked in the shins. 3 on 1 were dirty odds, but if they were gonna fight dirty, he would too. Trying to get the blood out of his mouth, Mike looked up and saw a prime target. He caught another punch to the shoulder blade, and in a moment of instinctual and guttural, adrenaline-laden reaction, uppercut one of his attackers right in the crotch. The tall kid made a squealing noise like a little pig who was terrified of a coming butcher and went down, his face slamming against the seats.

Mike backed up from the other two attackers and looked up, one was coming right for him. Using his basketball instincts he stepped aside as the momentum carried the shortest of the three kids past him and sent him shoulder-first into a pole. When Mike looked up the other attacker was driving his first towards him. Mike prepared to take another punch, his mind was ready, there was no way of dodging this one. He shut his eyes.

There was a whooshing sound, and then a sound of a punch, but it wasn't to his face. He opened his eyes to see the other attacker down. There was a figure in his peripheral and he began to turn to see what was going on when suddenly the figure next to him went down to the ground. The recovered attacker who just went flying into the pole came from behind, tackling the figure around the knees.

Mike felt dizzy, not knowing what was going on, so he stood back for a second to observe. The tall kid was still lying on the ground face down on the floor, whimpering, holding on to his nuts. The one who was about to punch him was sprawled out on the floor, face down, rising slowly and just trying to get his bearings. Whoever this figure was, he was not one of the attackers. He was helping. Mike had to help back. He grabbed the short attacker by the shoulders and dragged him backward. The tackled figure was trying to get up on the floor. Mike dragged the attacker further back, freaking out the remaining passengers behind them, and shoved him to the floor in the opposite direction. He heard motion behind him, raised his fist, turned around getting ready to swing it forward, and met the last face he expected to see.

***

Mikell didn't expect to get taken down at the knees, so this move caught him off guard. He nearly collided with a corner of a seat, missing it with his head by mere inches. He tried to get up but the attacker was still holding on to his legs. As Mikell was about to kick away, his legs were suddenly free. He scrambled up to his feet, glancing behind him. He turned around to see that the kid he pulled others off of was disposing of the attacker who tackled him on the floor. Mikell adjusted his shirt and looked up as the kid was turning around. With a fist balled together, the face turned to him was wearing a mask of crimson, with wild eyes staring through it. Mikell blinked and then threw his hand up in the air as the first came flying at him. So much for helping!

***

Mike's fist stopped short of its target. He shook his head to make sure what he was seeing in front of him was real. Mikell Sharp?? Here?? Of all the faces in the world, this was the last one he ever expected to see. Mike blinked to make sure he was not imagining things because of a concussion or something that the attackers gave him with that beating.

He was about to speak when he saw the kid that Mikell clearly knocked out to help him get up and pull something from his jacket pocket. Mike looked Mikell in the eyes and then dove down at the kid planting his knee firmly on the kid's wrist. The kid groaned in pain as Mike felt his wrist go limp. An unopened switchblade fell out. Thinking quickly, Mike grabbed it and slid it as far as he could across the train floor. He got good distance as the blade shot off several dozen feet, landing under a set of seats significantly far away.

Mike pressed his knee harder on the fallen kid's wrist, being quite aware that he had already injured him, but not caring. And then something hit him in the face, blurring his vision and sending more blood spilling from his nose.

**

The last of the idiots had clearly been the smartest of the bunch. He hung back observing the action. He wasn't too scared to get involved it seemed, but rather he was a wily, shameless opportunist who saw his shot and took it. He kicked Mike square in the head, then turned his attention to Mikell. Mikell couldn't react quickly enough as the kid turned around and sucker-punched him square in the jaw. Mikell rocked backward almost falling on the two guys behind him. One was on his phone trying to get a hold of the cops, while another was able to brace against Mikell falling, and pushed off.

The sudden shift from the back sent Mikell forward right towards the kid who just punched him. He almost took his eyes off Mikell considering helping his knocked-down friends. But upon seeing Mikell reeling back at him, he planted the steel-toed boot he was wearing into Mikell's stomach. Mikell doubled over and collapsed on his knees as his air evacuated from his lungs. The kid lifted his foot to stomp down on Mikell but got yanked backward by his belt by Mike who had just turned and regained his bearings. The kid stumbled back with Mike's ankle being right behind him and tripped backward.

Mike got up and stood over the kid, realizing that suddenly the situation was turning bleak. Mikell was still on the floor holding his gut, while all 4 of their attackers were nearly back up on their feet. Mike reached out for Lucia, who had been on one of the seats, screaming at everyone to stop fighting. She hesitated to take his hand, but got down and got behind him again. A young man standing behind Mike, who was not part of the fight nor was willing to be motioned for Lucia to get behind him as well to keep her out of harm's way. Mike stepped in front of Mikell. The tallest idiot was up and went right at Mike.

Mike could hardly see or breathe with his surely broken nose bleeding profusely all over the place. But he ducked and drove his shoulder into the attacker, pushing him back. He immediately felt punches to his back and kidneys by the others. Six violent pairs of fists pounded him to his knees and made him question his move. Then two of the fists were gone, then another two.

Mikell wasn't a fan of Mike's since the BNBL. Their experiences together had not led to anything that he would regard as enjoyable. Their conflict got them punished together, and Mike had only critiques about his ball skills. But now he instinctively felt like protecting his teammate. He didn't have the time to question why he felt this urge, but he was in it now, and it's not time to overthink things in the middle of a brawl. When he was able to get up he saw Mike fend off one of the kids and the others pounced on him.

Mikell grabbed one of the attackers by the ankle, yanking hard enough to make him lose his balance, and slammed down onto his chest. Then Mikell got up and grabbed another, turning him around and punching him square in the face. The kid fell backward like a log, knocked completely out. The tall kid that had been pushed back by Mike was staring straight at him while trying to pry Mike off of him and trying to reach for Mikell.

But being pinned back up against the train doors didn't allow him to reach Mikell. Mikell gave him a cocky grin and punched him right in the center of his face. The kid's head bounced back so hard that the back of it hit the train doors. When he looked back up, he had blood pouring down his forehead. Mikell punched him again and the kid buckled at the knees.

Mike felt him go limp and let go, turning his attention to the fourth attacker who was just turning around to confront Mikell. He received a kick to the side before he could turn, and then Mikell got a forearm to the ribs. This kid was willing to fight them both. The attacker who Mikell tripped up earlier was up now too and he threw his body at Mikell to tackle him. It didn't quite work but it made Mikell stumble enough to move away. Mike dove to tackle the kid, almost missing him. As they both landed on the floor and Mikell was propelled into the side seats the train began to slow down. The attacker felt the stop and got up quickly shoving away from Mike. He turned and dragged his knocked-out friend who was just coming back around, back to his feet. The other two were dragging themselves up as well.

The train stopped and the doors opened. A platform of passengers eager to get on the train reeled backward in the shocking display that they saw. 3 bloody kids and one with his sleeve partially torn off were getting up from what looked like a pool of blood in the middle of the train car. The crowd began to shout for cops, so the attackers began to head off through the open doors making their way into the crowd who was more than eager to get out of their way.

Mikell pushed himself off the seats and looked around. He saw the kids limping off the car. He felt his pocket for his phone. He would be pissed if it was broken. Then he turned to Mike who seemed to be aware that the fight stopped and was looking backward to find Lucia. She pushed her way to him and knelt down, crying her eyes out. She then glanced up at Mikell who was standing over them.

"The cops are coming!' - yelled a passenger from the far end of the car. The man who was shielding Lucia tapped Mike on the shoulder.

"Those assholes started this shit, you got like two dozen witnesses. We got you!" - he confidently said.

"Best we don't hang around to find out if they will believe them." - Mike heard from behind. He turned his head to see Mikell stretching out his arm, covered in blood, signaling that he was reaching out to help Mike to his feet. The last thing Mike needed now was to deal with cops, with all the shit going on at home, this would break his mother for sure. Looking at

Mikell's arm again, Mike stretched his hand out, and the two clasped bloody hands. Mikell yanked Mike off the floor and nodded to Lucia.

"We gotta go, man. Like yesterday!" - Mikell said. Mike nodded in agreement and the two boys, along with Lucia took off from the train doors. The crowd was already separating from the cops coming from the right side of the platform, so they cut left immediately and made a b-line for the nearest exit.

Chapter 16

Mike, Mikell, and Lucia skirted around the people at the busy T-station. They drew a lot of eyeballs, and many cell phones went up to people's ears as well as in front of their faces with their cameras facing toward the clearly hurting crew making their way out of the station. They darted out of sight as fast as they could once they cleared the station. It was hard to avoid notice with two bleeding dudes and a girl with her face covered in dried tears and running makeup. They looked like they just escaped from Leatherface after meeting the business end of his chainsaw.

Once they were far enough away they ran, or at least as much as Mike could run considering his current state. His shirt served as a means to stop his bleeding nose, though the result was simply a soaked shirt that left him nothing to wear besides it. When they were far enough away Mikell pointed to an old Boston side street, one too thin to fit a contemporary vehicle, but enough for a group of people to go into a dark area and figure out their next move.

The sirens from the train station were audible, but they had hoped that they avoided being detected by any passersby. Mikell wore his hood and Mike put the back end of his shirt over his head. Lucia tried to stay close to the two of them to avoid being recognized too. All she could think about was that her mom's worries were coming true in front of her and she would never hear the end of this after tonight.

Mikell finally thought to check his phone. As he expected there were texts from Isaiah. He didn't bother reading them now, he had a pretty good feeling he knew what the content would be. He kept looking around, recognizing how the scene looked. Anyone passing by, who would take even a double take into the side alley would realize that there were three figures there, and with any type of lighting, the observer would see that one was a walking bloodstain, one was a young lady in distress, and the other was a taller, hooded black man. He knew without a second thought what type of assumption that would draw. He did not doubt it. The times have changed, but they didn't change that dramatically.

Mike had a million things running through his dizzy mind. The first was that he needed to stay out of any entanglement with the law since that would be the last thing his family needed. The second was to deal with this bloodied face and nose. As Lucia dug in her purse for anything resembling tissues, Mike finally has something to stuff in his nostrils. If his nose broken, somehow he expected to be in significantly more pain, but mostly it was just the bleeding he was trying to stop. Maybe it was the adrenaline. Or maybe, he got extremely lucky and his nose was not broken after all. He leaned his head back against the wall, both nostrils full of tissues, and tried to process what the hell he had just gone through.

The sirens still rang out in the distance and there was a visible commotion in the area. Mikell knew that the longer they hung out there, the worse it would be. Eventually, they would draw the attention they were trying to avoid. They bailed from the train just a stop too early so they were not that far from the Paradise Rock Club. If they could find a way to get there discreetly, maybe he could get Isaiah to help them out. There would be questions, but getting into a concert full of people would not only help escape their current gritty situation but would also allow them to blend into a crowd in a dark place of relative anonymity where the eyes would be on the stage and not on them. Not to mention a mental escape, which everyone thoroughly needed, especially at this point.

 "How is your face?" - asked Mikell finally catching his breath.

 "Feels as good as your fists do." - Mike responded glancing down.

Mikell looked down at his blood-soaked hand and rubbed it realizing that the punches thrown took a serious toll on his bones. This was his shooting hand too. Maybe he should have stayed out of this whole thing. Would this screw him up on the court?

"Look, we can't just hang around here. Cops'll be canvassing the area looking for us as well as those bitches on the train. We need to get somewhere. Can you still get to where you were going?" - Mikell asked.

"I doubt they'd let us into any restaurant with me looking like this. And the bouncers at the show will turn me away too ....and call the cops while doing so." - Mike mumbled, frustrated.

"You going to a show? Where at?" - Mikell asked.

Mike hesitated. Mikell already knew he was into rap, but saying he was going to a concert was going to go to an area of impression and discussion Mike didn't feel like getting into, certainly not at the moment. Lucia didn't share his concerns though, so she spoke up when he kept quiet.

"Paradise Rock Club, there is a rapper performing we were gonna check out. But now..." - she trailed off.

"....Sleepy Hollow..." - Mikell said.

Mike looked from having his head tilted back. "You keeping tabs on the local rap scene like this all the time? That's gotta be a lot of work."

"No, wise ass. I'm going to the same show. My boy is waiting for me, blowin' up my phone because I'm not

164

there. Shit...I gotta get in touch with him." - Mikell realized he shouldn't put this off any longer and reached for his phone.

Mike considered the odds of this timely occurrence. "Same school, same team, same plans for the night, same train...never was big on cosmic level coincidences but holy shit....this is too much to overlook. Hey....hey, Mikell..."

Mikell was trying to read Isaiah's texts, but hearing his name he turned back around to Mike. "Yeah...?"

"You could have just let me have my ass beat back there. Lancing would have booted me from the team I'm sure, and you'd have all the glory. You were there by chance and didn't have to do shit, could have just stepped off the T and gone on with your life as almost everyone else on that train did. But you came in and got your ass kicked along with me. We did get some good shots in though, so....."

"He is trying to say, thank you for helping out. He knows you didn't have a dog in this fight." - Lucia finished his thought for him.

Mike looked over at her surprised, then closed his eyes and nodded. "Yeah...what she said. I don't know why you stepped in, but I appreciate you having my back."

Mikell put his phone down, letting the hand that was holding onto it hang down by his side. "Yeah, I didn't really know it was you till I got close. If some kid was getting their ass beat like that I would have done something anyway. When I saw that it was you, I thought I'd wait to see how you do when faced off against a squad. Then it occurred to me that you already did...yesterday on the court, and held your own. We have some history, and I still don't think you're easy to like. But you and I are on the same squad, so if I don't have your back, I'm not doing my job as a teammate. And those assholes needed a good beating anyway." He smirked, and Mike returned the smirk.

"So what are we gonna do?" - Lucia asked.

Mikell thought for a moment. He then put his phone in his pocket and pulled off his hoodie, and handed it to Mike. "Try not to get more blood on it. Throw your bloody shirt away, just tuck it deep into a dumpster so no one questions it. I got more layers, and I'll figure shit out. Let me hit my boy up. If you will settle for fast food for dinner instead, I think I could get us into that concert without problems."

Mike and Lucia exchanged a look. She shrugged. "You still up for that?"

Mike didn't have to think about it. "I came out for more than just a fight on a train." - he smiled through blood-soaked teeth.

Mikell put his phone to his ear and stepped a few feet away. Mike looked out into the street. People were passing by but no one was really looking over at them. He pulled his bloody shirt off, crumbled it into a ball, and put it on the ground next to him. Then he put on Mikell's hoodie, being careful to not let it touch his face. The blood flow was slowing down, and his nose still hurt, but if it was broken, Mike was surprised that it didn't hurt more. Could he have lucked out at least in this sense?

Lucia was trying to fix her eye makeup that had run down with her tears in a small mirror from her purse, turning constantly to catch some lighting from the main street next to them. She overheard Mikell quietly talking on the phone.

After a couple of minutes, Mikell hung up. He turned around and walked back over to them. The look on his face was far too delighted to resemble someone who just got disappointing news.

"You all wanna go meet Sleepy Hollow?" - he asked, raising his eyebrow.

Chapter 17

After handing Mikell ten bucks to run into a nearby CVS, Mike got his hands on some more tissues, rubbing alcohol, and an ice-cold Pepsi that allowed him a chance to first press it as a cold element against the multiple bruises he was sure to have, and then a drink that he was finding he very badly needed. Mikell also brought them a few slim jims, a couple of bags of chips, and some pretzels. They were ravenous, so this would do for dinner.

Lucia helped to tend to some of the cuts around his face by using the rubbing alcohol quickly. This was quite a predicament. The alcohol hurt like hell on the open gashes, but he had to bite his tongue to avoid seeming like a punk in front of Lucia. He got the sense that she totally picked up on his trying to tough it out, and began to hint that he didn't need to do that for her. Mikell paced around at the edge of the alley, anxiously looking around for any potential cops that might still be looking for kids from the fight on the train.

In a few minutes, Mike, dressed in Mikell's hoodie was ready to go. Mike's own shirt found a way into a nearby dumpster, which when opened confirmed for Mike that his nose still worked quite fine when he smelled the putrid scent that exited. Mike threw the hood over his head and he and Mikell, who seemed to not show his bruises or wounds too much started out through the street, with Lucia holding Mike's hand. This was not how Mike envisioned this going but he would take it.

They walked quickly through the brisk Boston air, trying to get to the Paradise Rock Club where Isaiah was waiting on the corner to take them around back. Mikell knew Isaiah was less than thrilled with the load he just dropped on him in the phone call, but once they got in there and met Sleepy Hollow, he was sure everyone would be too psyched to think about what happened before. Or so he hoped.

***

Isaiah paced nervously outside the side entrance to Paradise Rock Club, looking up to get the weary eye of security guards at the door. Two tour buses, one for Sleepy Hollow, the other for his opening performer that night, idled outside the club. After the phone call from Mikell, however, he wanted that time to come as late as possible.

All the arrangements he made, and now they wouldn't even make it here on time. Plus, Mikell was in a fight, with some white boy against a bunch of punks on the T, and who knows what shape they would show up in. Isaiah didn't anticipate getting Sleepy several people to meet so his confidence was shaken and his nerves were on edge. He hated feeling like this, this was a night to let loose and forget about the world for a while, but instead, here he was thinking he was doing a solid for Mikell, and the situation was quickly growing out of hand.

He glanced at his phone repeatedly, then looked around. Any second now he would be asked what his business was, and things would have to get awkward. He could see the line to the club inching past the edge of the building with people blocking off the side street, waiting to get in. Where the fuck is this kid??

***

A few blocks away from the club Mike was already a third through his Pepsi bottle. His body felt like hell, making him wonder if he was in a fight or just got done fending off a pack of starving wolves. His head still throbbed and his nose felt tender. He tried to suck it up and power through the pain. He couldn't exactly bring himself to let Lucia see him act the way he actually felt.

Tomorrow morning there would be a lot of explanations to be handed out when his parents saw his face. Ironically, in this case, telling the truth was his best bet. He stood up for his girl and got jumped...that's honorable shit! But wait till the coach sees him! Mike suspected his ass would get kicked all over again for that one. But he was willing to do all that as long as he could dodge police involvement.

Fat chance of that though; half a dozen people on that train were recording the fight with their phones. That video is probably achieving viral status now. Well, what was he going to do? It was what it was. The most concerning thing was that he suspected this would get to Lucia's mother, she would be proven that she was right to worry about her daughter, and then that will shut this blooming relationship right down.

With all of that on his mind, Mike nearly walked into Mikell's back as he was lost in thought with this hood on looking at the ground. Lucia's hand yanking him back was what stopped him.

"Hang here a minute..." - Mikell said, and he quickly walked over to the side street next to Paradise Rock Club. They were here, Mike didn't even realize it.

***

"........ah shit man, you were not bullshittin me! You look like you just met the business end of a baseball bat!" - Isaiah said throwing his hands up in the air dramatically.

"Yeah, but....keep it down. I know, it has been a weird fucking day for more reasons than I can even get into right now. Look I got the kid...Mike....he is on my squad. I didn't know he was getting his ass kicked, but

I had to get in there. Was four on one, they were messing with his girl. Anybody needs help with those numbers. He's going to the same show and we are trying to stay low-key. If you think I look like I met a baseball bat, he looks like he juggled chainsaws....badly! I let him go through the front door, he is going to get questions and looks that neither one of us can put up with right now. We need anonymity and cover. So I was thinking he can come in to meet Sleepy too. Even if the cops show up here looking for him, he won't be in the club to be found." - Mikell tried to plead his case on behalf of Mike, something he was still not entirely cognizant of being comfortable with.

"Well....shit...I mean, I hear ya...I guess. I dunno how this will play out. Could go to shit, but I'll try. No promises." - Isaiah took a deep breath.

"I know man, we'll take what we can get here" - Mikell answered appreciatively. Isaiah started walking to the tour buses. - "Hey....thanks, man!" - Mikell called out after him.

***

Mikell walked back over to Mike and Lucia. They looked up as he tapped his head up and nodded over to the buses.

"So you want to get us current on this plan of yours?" - Mike asked

"That back there is my old homie Isaiah. He has a cousin who....long story, but he has a connection to Sleepy Hollow. The kind where we, well....I, got invited to meet him backstage, possibly see the show from the side of the stage or some shit. With all the people recording our fight, we are not going to be anonymous for long, so I figured there is no reason to start the shit tonight. And since you are here, I tried to get you in there with me. Isaiah is jittery as shit over there having to go in and ask." - Mikell explained

"Damn...that's fucking epic! But...." - Mike hesitated, "why are you doing this for us? Saving me from getting my ass kicked so we didn't tank the season with just you playing is one thing but...."

"Whoa...who said it would be a tanked season with just me? Are you forgetting about the other 10 kids on that team? Just when I think maybe you are more straight up, you say some conceited shit like that. And who's to say you don't go down with a broken leg next game and then we go on to win the whole thing anyway?" - Mikell spat back, mildly offended.

"I'm sure that's not what he was saying..." - Lucia started.

"Not what I meant, you are twisting my words." - Mike sounded offended at the idea.

173

"Nah, I'm just hearing them. Look I'm giving you the benefit of the doubt here. My boy is in there trying to get you in, save you the trouble of being seen in your condition, drawing attention, and still being able to enjoy the show you just got your ass kicked coming to see. Don't make me feel like I shouldn't bother." - Mikell shot back.

"Guys... it's cool, ok?.... There is no need for this, let's just have a good time...or as good of a time as we can considering you are both beat up and my clothes are soaked and ruined." - Lucia interjected.

Mike looked at Mikell silently and nodded. Mikell shrugged and turned around to check for any activity off the tour bus. He saw nothing, so he turned back. Seconds later Mike and Lucia stood up straighter and Mikell heard jogging footsteps approaching from behind. He turned to see Isaiah running up to them.

Isaiah tilted his head quickly backward once he realized Mikell saw him as he approached. When he came up, he looked Mike up and down. "Shit son, you weren't foolin! This kid looks like shit!"

Mikell tried to redirect. "Yeah, Isaiah, this is Mike, Lucia... what's good?"

Isaiah looked at Mike questionably then said to Mikell while still looking at Mike. "He cool?"

Mikell glanced at Mike as if to be sarcastic. "Yeah....he cool...enough." - Mikell smirked.

"Well, it's your lucky day white boy.....Sleepy got another white boy in there, old-time friend or somethin' from way back. I heard he got Sleepy some studio time for demos or some shit before he made it, so they are tight. Sounds like he is cool with another white face in the room, but uh....not on the bus. When the crowd starts filing in, that's what he comes in the back of the club to keep the eyes off him. That will be happening soon, and he got a room back there, so you two will be welcome inside." - Isaiah explained.

Mikell was excited and nervous. He could tell Mike was too, but while Mikell hid his feelings, Mike tried to cover them up with bravado. "Sounds sweet!" - Mike exclaimed.

"I'm gonna wait by the door, when he comes out, I'll signal, you come over, but don't be getting anyone's attention from the line into the club, just real chill like." - Isaiah stressed.

"Yeah man....sure..."- Mike came back.

"Thanks man....cacan't wait." - Mikell said more discreetly.

Isaiah nodded, casting another look at Mike's face, and jogged back over to the side of the building. "Shit looks painful..."

Chapter 18

The experience that Mike and Mikell shared on the night of the concert was surreal before they got to the show, but their experience there broke the reality barrier altogether. Isaiah led Mike, Mikell, and Lucia past the super-muscular man in front of the club's back door. Isaiah nodded to him, and the big guy nodded back, ever-so-slightly. They entered a small hallway that twisted on a curve that eventually straightened to reveal a 20-foot hall with multiple doors on both sides. The one at the far end was open with voices of a party-like atmosphere eminating from within.

An even bigger security guy stood in front of the door. Mike, Mikell, and Lucia could hear the bass pumping, but they couldn't tell if it was coming from the room up ahead or not. Once they reached the doorway, they realized that it was, but it was also reverberating on the walls, as the beat was being pumped into the club as well to entertain the gathering crowd. Isaiah cautiously slowed as he approached the door. The big guy in front held up his hand and took a look inside the doorway. Someone inside said something, and the guy peeked back out and waved them in.

Isaiah turned to look at the crew, raised his eyebrows, and turned to lead them in. The room wasn't overly large, though a bit crowded. Two twins stood over in the corner talking to a shorter man with dreadlocks, and several scantly dressed women in mini-skirts and low cut dresses sat drinking what looked like glasses of white wine on the couch. A man dressed in a suit stood in the corner talking to someone on the phone. Off in the corner, a figure sat staring at his phone, while a gorgeous black girl who was wearing far more makeup than her pretty face required, sat on his leg.

Mike and Mikell immediately recognized him as Sleepy Hollow. They stopped short in the room until Isaiah headed over to the short man in the corner. The guy turned as Isaiah approached and nodded to him. The guy looked at Isaiah with a smile then had the smile fade when he looked at the new arrivals to the room. He glanced back at the twins, said something, they nodded, and he headed over to Mike, Mikell, and Lucia. They expected a whole set of rules about not talking to Sleepy at all or touching anything, but the man strolled over and addressed them all with a first bump.

"I heard you had some trouble tonight boys. Should we have paramedics on standby or are they busy reviving the other guys?" - he smiled mischievously.

Mike smirked, while Mikell lowered his head to laugh.

"Yeah, there we go. Them be the faces we wanna see. You're at a concert, if you are not here in a good mood and to have fun, you wandered into the wrong place. Anyways, I heard the cliff notes version from Isaiah of your adventures tonight. But I wanna hear more about how the fuck you two ended up here, together. Cuz.....uh....let's just say I've been to the BNBL so I know who you two are. And no...yo boy here, didn't mention that we got two riot causing hooligans coming onto the premises." - he glanced back to Isaiah, who looked confused. "Sleepy just wants to perform tonight fellas, he doesn't need the cops showing up here, busting up the gig, looking for two legit ass-kicking ballers. That gonna be a problem?"

Mike glanced at Mikell as if he wanted him to field the awkward question. Mikell hesitated, but then nervously said: "Nah...we got outta there fast. No one saw us come here and we...."

The short man turned to Isaiah. "This dude gave up all his humor for his balling skills in some deal with the devil or somethin'?"

Isaiah snickered. Mike, caught on to the joke, tried not to laugh, but heard Lucia giggling behind him and had to smile. Mikell was a second late to get the joke, and felt a bit embarrassed, but masked it with a nodded head and a head shake.

The short man laughed. "Now we good, now we good. Aight you wanna sit down? I get you something to drink." He pointed to the couch next to the two women, as one of them suggestively waved her finger at Mikell. "Yo Sleepy, got some fans up in here for when you feel like talking." - he shouted. Then he turned back to Mike and Mikell. "I'm T by the way. Those two knuckleheads in the corner are Jold and Jong. Terrible pun for an act, I know, they will never make it on their skills with that name. They are Hollow's openers, they go up in a few. You boys hang, relax when Hollow goes up, you come to watch with me from the side of the stage...yeah?"

Before anyone had a chance to say another word, T scooted passed them and skirted out of the room. At that moment, the bathroom door opened on the side of the room, and a white-skinned man in his late 20s stepped out, zipping his pants. He looked around the room and when his eye fell on Mike and Mikell he stopped short and squinted his eyes.

"Oh, shit....no way!" He let his shirt down and came right over. "This is crazy, you are who I think you are?? I watched that riot man, and I don't care what they say, I don't think you started it. People were just looking to jump. You just got caught up in the moment."

Not eager to relive the events of the BNBL, Mike and Mikell just shook their heads in agreement.

"Dope for y'all to join us all. Good to have fresh faces, otherwise it's the same crew rotating on through here." He turned. "Yo Sleep, you gonna keep being antisocial Sasha over there in the corner, or you gonna come and meet your guests?"

***

A very surreal hour and a half later, Sleepy Hollow hit the stage to a booming round of cheers from the club. He went right into his first song as Mike, Mikell, and Lucia came up to the side of the stage and T sent for someone to get them some chairs. Talk about a premium view! They sat down for a couple of songs but Mikell couldn't help looking out at the crowd so he got up and inched closer to the stage.

Mike looked over at Lucia, who got the sense that he wanted to see the live crowd too. She smiled and nodded towards the stage. He smiled back and headed up standing next to Mikell. The show was a straight sellout and Sleepy played banger after banger, with the crowd loving every moment. They could literally see the heads bopping to the beat. Sleepy went into his next jam which got a roar from the crowd and Mike and Mikell both were psyched to hear this song. They both found themselves rapping along with Sleepy, getting more animated by the moment. Lucia covered her face to hide her laughter.

And then...Sleepy turned to their side of the stage and his gaze caught them getting into the music. When he polished off the verse...he waved the DJ off and the beat lowered. Then he turned to the crowd and asked where the Boston basketball fans were and the crowd popped. So he asked who has seen the BNBL and the riot that followed. The crowd returned with a scattering of confused cheers and boos.

Sleepy then went on to say: "Then you might know my two guests tonight. They stopped by after giving out some ass whoopings earlier, and not to each other this time. They dealt with a few punk-ass bitches on the train trying to mess with my man Mike's girl. Y'all wanna meet 'em?"

The crowd roared approvingly, at which point Sleepy turned to the side of the stage and pointed to Mike and Mikell, then pointed next to him on the stage. It took the boys a second to register what was going on. He was inviting them on stage with him? This is ridiculous. Mike found himself shaking his head no, only to feel Mikell smack his arm, and turning to him he found a look of bewilderment only to be nearly pushed out to the stage by Mikell.

Mikell was in some sort of trance. He must have gotten punched in his head way too hard because he was clearly laying on the train, dreaming that this was happening. To him. Right now. With...Mike at his side?? Yup, definitely out cold on the train, no doubt about it. Mikell was convinced. But while he was dreaming he might as well dream hard. And as long as this is a dream, they don't have to worry about any bystanders recognizing them from the train or the videos that were surely going viral by now.

Before either one of them could blink an eye they were sharing a stage with Sleepy, and he waved over to the opposite end with his fist. "Yo, I be spittin' up here, and I see the two spittin' from the sides and I see this two droppin' lines with me. So why not do it with me up here. Yo, hand these boys some mics, hook 'em up!"

The crowd went nuts. "Come on... let's do this, let's go from the top." Sleepy said and spun his finger around in the air as if signaling the DJ to restart the song. The beat dropped again and Sleepy led off with the first verse. When he reached the transition for the hook, he stepped back and pointed to Mikell.

As if was instinctual, Mikell continued rapping from that part, and when he got to the next verse, he glanced over to Sleepy who was pointing at him and the crowd. The next thing he knew, the crowd faded into his hearing over the beat which seemed to be the only thing he was hearing the entire time one stage until then. They were losing their minds. Mikell was looking for some signal of what to do next, when none came, he just went into the next verse. The crowd cheered harder, and when the verse ended, Mikell took his eyes off the bright spotlights and glanced at Sleepy who was nodding and then pointed to Mike.

Mike knew something like this was coming but still felt caught off guard. He quickly glanced to the side as Lucia was waving to him to roll with it. So he did. He spit the next hook and without ever looking at Sleepy, went straight for the next verse. The crowd was still roaring. When he reached the next and final part, he suddenly heard Mikell's voice join, and then Sleepy's. They were rapping in unison...on stage...together! What world was Mike living in?

The crowd was going nuts, as was Lucia. Mike even forgot about the fact that all the bopping and bouncing he started doing, shook loose the blood from his nose, and it began to drip all over Mikell's hoodie. He was so into the song that it startled him when a towel flew in from his side and landed on his shoulder. The song ended and Mike glanced at the towel, then realized what was going on, he put the microphone down and realized it looked like he was bowing to the crowd.

"Take a bow brotha....you earned that shit! Yo, Mike and Mikell people! Give it up! If their ballin' future don't pan out, try the rap game!" - Sleepy said.

Mikell got the hint that its time to get off the stage, but Mike was in full wanderlust mode. Mikell shifted closer to him, waved to the crowd, and nudged Mike along, knocking him out of his trance. Mike quickly got the hint, and put his fist up to the crowd, then put the towel on his blood-red nose. The two walked off stage together to a round of resounding cheers while Sleepy got the crowd into his next jam.

Lucia was so excited she put away her phone which she was using to record what just happened and jumped to give Mike a giant hug. Her shoulder pressed against the towel on his nose, sending a jolt of pain through his head and his ears, but he wasn't going to push her away. She quickly realized and backed off, covering her mouth, then taking her hands away and mouthing "sorry" as she let her excitement overtake her.

Mikell realized he was holding his breath as if exhaling will make all of this not real anymore. He looked over at Mike and Lucia who glanced at him, and he felt himself smile. He wanted to play it cool but he couldn't help it. This dream was just too good.

"Y'all be trending tomorrow. Shed some blood on stage with Sleepy, shit you are gonna be local legends. For the right reasons this time!" - Isaiah shouted at them from 15 feet away and winked sarcastically.

***

Mike was elated. If only he had known what this surreal dream sequence he was living would result in. He knew in the back of his mind that he would need to explain to his parents what happened to his face. He knew that there was no escaping someone coming across the video from the train, but he thought he could deal with that. He would even find a way to deal with Lancing and whatever repercussions that came from the fight. Hell, he felt on top of the world, and he would even talk his way out of this with the cops if it came to it.

He only wished that he asked Lucia to not post the video of him rapping on stage with Sleepy. That would have saved him some serious headaches in the days to come...

Chapter 19

After a night that felt like some sort of dream, Mike basically forgot about his physical shape. His nose stopped bleeding and the excitement of the show plus his big stage appearance and being able to rap in front of the crowd was exhilarating. That night certainly started out shitty, but not only did he solidify a friendship with Mikell, the last person he ever imagined he would befriend, but he made Lucia unfathomably happy, and her elation spurred more of his own.

The adrenaline kicked in...hard. There was very little that could have bothered him. Even when the thoughts of all the questions that would be asked of him came about in his mind, he brushed them aside. Mike figured those could all be worries for another day because he was living a dream, and it was one he had no desire to wake up from.

They all got backstage passes signed by Sleepy, as well as Jold and Joung, the opening act twins who were eager to get their names out there in the world. The autographed passes were lamented backstage and were treated like some kind of precious metal as Mike and Mikell both carried them out of the club.

The three made their way back to the final trains leaving the area and hopped on board a (thankfully) only partially occupied car, mostly filled with people leaving bars and shows in the area. Most of them were too drunk to be upright for more than a few seconds, a couple of girls fell asleep leaning on each other's shoulders, and one guy was off sleeping off a drunken stupor in the corner, drool streaming from his lip, while his annoyed-looking female counterpart tried to lose herself in her phone screen.

Mike and Mikell chatted about the concert, forgetting for the moment that just a few days ago they still had nothing but an uneasy alliance mostly relegated to the basketball court. Mike recognized this fact, and he was fine with it. Mikell knew it was happening too, but he wasn't going to make things awkward by getting all insightful about their sudden bond. Both boys knew that of all the things they could have predicted would happen that night, no matter how outlandish, there is no way either one of them foresaw this as the result.

Lucia showed the boys the video, which elicited laughs from all three, Mikell told them that he wasn't sure what took him over, but he just felt right being on stage. Maybe his days of being at the center of the courts surrounded by screaming fans had him used to the atmosphere. Though the nature of what he did was far different than what he actually did that night. Mike thought that he looked like some kind of crackhead that got up on stage to audition for the drill rap version of American Idol. Lucia assured him that he rocked the performance and that people are going to love seeing this. She thought that he would watch it back years later and remember that as a night not when he got into a fight and got bloodied up, but when he had a dream-like experience.

Mike was just too excited and riding the high of the night to realize that when Lucia said people would adore the video, it meant people would see it, and that would open up a whole can of worms he didn't expect in his life. Mikell didn't even consider the fact that he was also in the video, continuing the chat about the night with gleeful excitement.

***

Mikell hopped off first, while Mike and Lucia took the train two more stops, and they got off at a hub point to switch to another train to get to their stop. Mikell walked home through the brisk air, picking up pace as he was feeling legitimately cold. Mike still had his hoodie, and he needed to get back to his house. He could only hope that Pops was not waiting up for him. The questions he would get would not end, and honest answers would not go over well. Pops knew Mikell went out, but he rarely returned that late in the evening, so he would certainly have some explaining to do. But if Pops was asleep, Mikell could hope to quietly get to bed, and then he could claim he got home earlier than he did.

Luck continued to be on his side. He was a bit nervous when the kitchen light was still on, after all, Pops was not one to waste things, electricity included, but so was the TV. First Mikell thought he was about to get a talking to, but then he heard the sweetest sound of all: an elongated snore.

Quietly shutting the squeaky door, Mikell slipped off his sneakers and headed to his room where he changed clothes into a sleeping attire that was far warmer than he was used to, but the chill was strong with him after the walk from the train. He quietly headed back to the room where Travis was passed out in his chair, snoring delightfully away in his own slumber. Mikell's body was just calming after the night, but he told himself he needed to get all the rest he could. First, he had a game tomorrow, and second, any exhaustion and physical damage his body underwent would be easier to recover from if he fully rested.

He knew he would have a tough time falling asleep, but he would have to force himself to do so. He snuck by Pops and slid the remote from his grasp, then turned off the TV. He then took a throw blanket from the couch and put it over Pop's lap. He then snuck back through the kitchen, turning the lights off. He headed back to his bedroom, quietly closing the door, plugging his phone in, and bringing up the alarm app. He would allow himself to sleep just a bit more, but he had to get up and get ready for his game. He set an alarm at a time reasonable by his estimation, turned off the screen, and set his phone down.

He got into bed and made himself comfortable. He then started thinking about the events of the night as he stared at the ceiling. Deciding he could do the same with his eyes closed, Mikell shut his eyes. Turns out, he was far more exhausted than he thought. The next thing he knew, his alarm was going off and it was bright outside. He genuinely felt like he only just blinked.

***

Mike and Lucia walked from the train to their cars as Lucia had an idea. She dug in her purse, pulled out her makeup kit, and opened it. Mike hesitated, but Lucia reminded him that people would be asking questions. Specifically, his parents would most certainly lose their minds if they were to see Mike covered in bruises and blood. She grabbed a makeup removed wipe and cleaned up the remaining dry blood around Mike's nose. She was not going to be able to fix the swelling around his nose and eyes, but it was encouraging that it got better since earlier in the night, and a semi-full night of sleep should help out even more.

Lucia then took out some foundation, and against Mike's pretentious insisted that he save a little bit of face (even now she was making puns), and have it look

190

not as bad as it was. She even suggested that he keep out of sight if he could, and ditch the hoodie. Mike reminded her of his game the next day, so he would not be able to hide his appearance for long. But he would take what he could get.

She applied the foundation to his face and told him not to wash it off. As an incentive, when she was done, she leaned over and kissed his cheek. "Now," she said with a sarcastic smile, "really don't wash it off." The two then parted, and while Mike wanted to kiss her, he thought better of a night where he had quite enough excitement. Lucia was hopefully not going anywhere and as long as she could pacify her mom about him being a good guy and maybe not meeting her mother till his current appearance had headed up, would be good for everyone.

***

Lucia headed back to her car, and Mike to his. When Lucia got in the car, she smiled and pulled out her phone while the car was heating up. Rewatching the video of Mike and Mikell made her smile, and she made a decision that seemed as benign as any other, she posted the video of them rapping with Sleepy on YouTube.

Lucia had all the best intentions. Mike was great and she just wanted him to get the recognition for not just being a solid ballplayer, but a halfway decent rapper too. Plus, there is the minor brush with fame. This moment needed to live on in the web-verse. Unfortunately for Mike, this was going to have a very different effect; it would be one that would bring trouble and frustration to his life.

***

Mike's head was a mix of thinking about his awesome night and how he would handle his parents at this late hour, looking like he did, wearing someone else's hoodie. He would need to be creative. His best possible scenario was that the house would be quiet and everyone would be asleep. His parents were people who went to bed pretty early as it is, so he was trying to tell himself that would be the case tonight too.

His final stroke of luck for a while was that he was right. He anticipated someone waiting for him, but in thinking about it, with all the crap they went through with his brother, Mike was the responsible one, so his parents could go to sleep relatively worry-free. Oh, if they only knew!

The house was quiet, with only the outside light and the hallway light staying on, clearly for Mike's convenience. He crept through the house quietly taking his sneakers off at the door. He successfully made it to his room and quickly got out of the hoodie, cringing as his shoulders and hands suddenly remembered that they were in pain. He decided to shove the hoodie down to the very bottom of his laundry basket and take care of it when he was home alone in the coming days. He headed to the bathroom to check himself out in the mirror. This was the first time he saw himself outside the dark lighting of the club in Lucia's video. This was not going to clear up in time for his game tomorrow. His body hurt and if he tried to play basketball in this shape, he would be utterly screwed.

Mike decided that the night was worth it and he would take things as they came. For tonight, he had only one mission, get to bed and recharge. He changed, rinsed off the still remaining dirt on his hands from being on the train floor earlier, and almost threw water on his face, realizing that he shouldn't be doing that. He wiped his hands and headed off to bed.

It was one of the best nights of sleep he had in some time. It would also be the last good sleep he'd have for a while...

Chapter 20

Mikell rolled out of bed, eager to inspect how he looked before he saw Pops. Even more importantly, he needed to know that his appearances would not draw questions from his team or his coach. Either way, the questions were unavoidable because the story of his altercation on the train with Mike was bound to hit the internet if it hadn't already, and someone was bound to recognize them from the club. Especially since Sleepy made it a point to say exactly who they were to the crowd.

Even if none of those things happened, the way Mike looked would certainly present plenty of questions, and it would pull Mikell in by proxy. Mikell was walking a fine line between riding the high of the previous night and feeling anxiety about the future. Part exhausted, part pumped for today's game, Mikell decided that he would use the opportunity to give his body a bit more time to heal as he threw on some clothes and carefully snuck out of his room. He didn't see Pops in the kitchen, so he moved to the front door.

"Pops, if you're awake, I'm running out for some breakfast. Bring you back anything?" - Mikell asked, his head already peeking out the door.

From the bathroom, he heard: "I'm good son, see you in a bit."

Mikell felt enormous relief. There seemed to be no suspicions from the typically hyper-aware Travis, and he was not around to see Mikell's outward appearance. Luckily, Mikell could mask most current problems under the hood of his hoodie. However, eating with Pops with a hoodie on might be suspect. That reminded him that he would need to figure out what to do with the one he gave Mike.

Mikell headed out and down the street. There was a bagel and donut placed on the corner, but he knew that would bring him home too quickly. He needed to get some more time in, so he headed to a breakfast diner seven blocks away. He planned to order food, then wait for it, and head home to eat it. He would figure the rest out later.

***

Mike could only wish that his morning was as tame as Mikell's started. Checking his face out in the mirror, Mike could see improvement. He didn't bother, until now to think about how he was going to explain this to either of his parents. His best bet was to say that there was a commotion at the concert that he got caught in the middle of, but his parents weren't cave-people. They kept up with news online, and eventually, the videos from the train would make it to them.

Maybe he should be honest. It would certainly give him less to hide later on. Besides, he would have enough problems with his coach, he was sure.

After carefully weighing his options, Mike grabbed some clothes and quietly left his room to go take a shower. He wanted to stretch his muscles a bit and exercise, to get prepped for the game, but his body was telling him to save his energy for game time. He was able to get through his 10-minute shower just fine, finding this to be the one safe place of solace. It gave him a feeling of ease. Things will get worse before they get better, he thought, but it will get better.

Once he stepped out of the shower and toweled off, he left the bathroom. His mother was in the hall and he quickly turned his head, but acknowledge her with a quick: "Hey ma."

"Hey there, what time did you get in? I was so tired that I clocked out early. How was your big date?" - she asked.

Mike slowly made his way to his room. "I was back pretty late, but gotta get going on my day for the game later. The date was good. Lucia is a great girl."

"Am I going to meet her?" - his mom asked, half-jokingly.

Not thinking, Mike turned to roll his eyes at which point the smile off his mother's face dropped as she saw his.

"Mike! What happened??" - she rushed over to him. "You look like you were mugged! Tell me, who did this!"

There was no point in lying, it would all come out later. Mike saw his brother start lying to his parents before, and then he had to lie to cover the lie, and so on and so on. Wasn't long before he couldn't keep the lies straight. Mike always told himself he wouldn't repeat the same mistakes, nor would he do that to his parents. They have dealt with enough.

"Ma, look, I'm fine ok. It looks way worse than it is. Some assholes spilled a drink on Lucia on the T, then they laughed about it. One thing led to another, and we...had words." - Mike said

"Those were some words, to leave bruises all over your face like that! Did you fight multiple boys for the girl you were on a first date with??" - she put her hands on his head and examined his bruises.

"Words might have been said by fists. There was a bunch of them and one of me....well, for a hot minute anyway. Turned out someone had my back, in the unlikeliest assist I could ever imagine." - Mike continued. "We did better than those bastards. Don't worry we didn't attract any unwanted attention. I hope not, anyway."

"Any injuries I can't see??" - his mom asked concerned.

"Sore all over but, nothing bad. Hurt my hands a bit busting their faces. My nose took the worst of it." - Mike replied.

At this point, Mike's father came up the stairs and stopped short to see the interaction. Typically a stoic man, he headed over Mike's way and stepped next to his mother.

"Jesus kid, you wander onto my construction site and get some hammers dropped on you?" - he asked sarcastically.

Before he had a chance to retort, Mike's mother answered for him: "He was standing up for his woman, and apparently that required provoking several boys into jumping him. Luckily someone helped out. I'm not sure if I should be furious or proud of your chivalry."

"You leave at least a broken bone?" - his father asked, drawing a stink-eye from his mother.

This was going better than Mike expected. "Maybe, kinda doubt it. A couple of them had a tough time getting back to their feet. But we got out of there before the cops showed and still made it to the show.

Had the best time too." Mike was not going to go into more details than that.

"You need to ice the hell out of your face before your coach sees you looking like a smashed blueberry. I'll grab you some from the freezer." With that, his father headed back down the stairs.

"And the girl, Lucia, how is she? Going to go out with you again after you got into a brawl on the first date?" - she asked.

"We had a great time besides that, so yeah, I think this has a chance. You ain't gonna embarrass me if you do meet her are you?" - Mike asked, only half-jokingly.

"Michael! I am your mother. How could you ask me such a thing? Of course, I'm going to embarrass you. It's part of my job as your mom. If I don't, I am screwing up this mothering thing worse than I thought." - she winked. "Look, please relax and ice your face. You have a few hours before the game. Hopefully, enough time to get the swelling down. Are you sure you're fine otherwise? Pulling out of the game may not be the worst thing for you."

"No mom, I'm good. I hear dad coming with the ice now, let me go take care of it." - Mike replied.

His mother nodded as his father ascended the stairs with three zip lock bags of ice the family kept in the freezer as additional cooling elements. He handed them to Mike and patted him on the shoulder, nodding his head with seeming approval. "Glad you're good. Hope those punks think twice about messing with people again. Hope they are wearing some bruises too."

Mike smirked, realizing it still hurt his nose to do so. He nodded to his father, looked at his mom, and headed back to his room to ice and get ready for the day.

"Mike....who was it that helped you out anyway?" - his mother asked as he was about to close his door.

Mike turned slightly. "You know Mikell from the squad? The one from the BNBL who is now playing on my team? Well..."

"Seriously??" - both of his parents asked at once.

Chapter 21

Mike expected a talking-to from Lancing when he got to the game, but he got quite a bit more than that. While he cleverly tried to hide his face under a hood and keep turned away from coach Lancing for as long as he could, Mike realized it was only a matter of time until he would have to face up to his appearance. The ice treatment did help a bit more, but at this point, it would take a miracle for everything to heal up in time. Hell, he would probably be sporting some marks on his face for next week's game too.

Lancing was already glancing at him with skeptical looks, making Mike wonder if he was aware of the videos from the train. Eventually, when Mike had to stretch and start warming up, the hoodie had to come off, and his hair was nowhere near long enough to hide anything. Where was Lucia with that foundation now? Though he would likely sweat it off on the court, look like a damned melting wax figure, and his luck would turn out for the worse. Maybe he was better off. But it was what it was, he knew he would need to deal with it eventually.

One look at his face and Lancing called his name, then waved him over. Lancing wasn't going to lambast one of his best players publicly, or any of his players really, but he was not going to let one of his guys be on the court looking like Mike was at the moment. Pulling Mike out into the hallway, Lancing questioned what the hell happened. Mike planned to come kind of clean, the same rationale he used with his parents, but lighter on the details. Lancing listened impatiently, then looked around to make sure no one was in earshot and told Mike exactly what Mike feared hearing.

Lancing was not going to have him on the court looking like he did. The questions that this would prompt would be a huge headache for them both, and the team. Lancing would rather chance it without one of his star players. Plus, he wasn't convinced that Mike would have the energy or the stamina during that game. After what happened, there is no way his mind was on the court. Mike wanted to argue, but he couldn't. Lancing was not wrong.

Where things got odder is when Lancing insisted that Mike ride the bench for the game and have a towel over his head. The goal was obviously to hide him from the eyes of the questioning crowd. Mike didn't see the logic. If he sat there with a towel over his head, and he was the only one doing so, he would stick out like a sore thumb. Lancing's point was that he would stick out more his questionable appearance was exposed. If Lancing sent him to the locker room, there would be even more questions about his whereabouts.

Mike realized that there were no good solutions, just varying degrees of annoying ones. He decided that he had caused enough trouble already with his appearance and he would concede to what Lancing wanted. He returned to the court as the crowd was steadily filing in, and grabbed two towels, throwing one over his head and the other over his lap. He planted himself on the far part of the bench.

As he peeked out from behind the towel trying to no show his face much, his blinder-like towel side was lifted by someone who dropped in the seat next to him. It was Asher.

"Shit man...how and why are you even here?" - Asher asked.

Mike pulled the towel back down over his head. His mood was already soured by the whole situation going on that he preferred not to be annoyed by anyone. "It's fine. It's just for the game. Anyway, I had a long night, not exactly full of energy right now."

"Getting your ass kicked by 4 hood rats will do that to a guy." - Asher quipped.

"Ah, shit...." thought Mike. Then he moved the side of the towel. "Video is everywhere then, ha? Figures. It was four on one and ..."

"Hey!" - Asher cut him off. "Couldn't have been that bad. You were up on stage with the same hood rats, making that tribal noise shit a few hours later. Yeah...caught that one too. My boy Mason, his girl got all the juice from your Ms. Chikita Banana too. All giddy about her big protector getting his 15 minutes of...."

Asher's verbal diarrhea was interrupted by being shoved backward by Mike who rose up, irate at what he just heard. Asher stumbled into the far end of the team's chairs and awkwardly rolled into the desk beyond them. Mike was on his feet, both towels on the floor, fists clenched and moving towards Asher.

"So fuckin tired of your mouth, you prick. I'm done pity friending you. Thought you were decent trying to be all friendly with me when I started here, but you showed your ignorant, racist attitude over and over. Your mouth was always gonna get your ass kicked, you pissant bitch, even if you didn't keep my name and my girl's name out of it, but I didn't think it was gonna be today."

As Asher stumbled to his feet Mike snapped back out of full-rage mode to realize that the gym noise had subdued and everyone was staring at him. He realized he was still moving forward. His body was driving him ready to throw down. Then a pair of players stepped up behind Asher who had just gotten back up to his feet. "Can't take a joke? You get some pointers from your team of voodoo doctors? Why don't you go reverse Michael Jackson yourself and join those thugs you love listening to so much."

Mike felt the rage grow and the care of who was watching fade. Suddenly a pair of hands wrapped around his waist. Then a big arm stuck in front of him, pressing him back on his chest. Mike blinked to see Mikell's face at his side, holding him back.

"Whatcha doin', man? You need a repeat of last night??" - Mikell said quietly, but loud enough to be audible to Mike's ear. "Ignore that little bitch...mind over matter. If you don't mind, he doesn't matter."

"I'm tired of his ass!" - Mike raise his voice significantly.

"I've been tired of him ever since he opened his mouth around me the first time. But this isn't about him. Chill! Things aren't hard enough after yesterday? You and the squad needs this kind of attention like you need a firecracker up your ass."

Mike was too determined to get to Asher. "You were on the right side of shit yesterday, don't jump to the wrong side now. - Mikell pressed him back harder, positioning his body in Mike's way, nearly obstructing Asher from view. As Mike was getting his wits about him, Asher had to keep poking the bear.

"Saving him again ha? Let him come at me, let him go! Makes you wonder who was getting defended on the train yesterday, ha princess?" - Asher said.

"The fuck'd you say?" - Mike was not actively shoving to get past Mikell who kept holding strong.

Suddenly, Lancing was there, between them and he glared at Mike with a look that signaled that he was not having this anymore. "Get your shit, and go back home to cool off! Now! We are gonna talk on Monday, Cassidy! Do not be in the locker room at halftime! Move!"

With that Lancing directed an assistant coach to escort Mike out of there. Mikell walked along with him, trying to get him to the door. Mike was even more furious now. Everyone saw his outburst and he was sure they would think now that the incident on the train went pretty much the same way. Not to mention that he was physical, so he would be viewed as the aggressor. Yet not everyone could hear the shit Asher said to him. This was total bullshit.

Mikell and the assistant coach walked Mike out to the parking lot once Mike grabbed the stuff out of his locker. He didn't even bother changing. "Coach, I got it from here, I'll be back in a couple. Can I handle this?" - Mikell pleaded. Mike, huffing, and puffing walked back and forth, his face redder than a tomato.

The assistant coach hesitated but realizing that Mikell probably would have more control nodded cautiously. "Cassidy. I'm not kidding when I say this: Lancing is not going to go lightly on you. Your best move is to do what he wants right now and calm the hell down. It's already a bad scene, don't make it worse for yourself." With that, he turned and walked back off.

***

After Mikell got Mike to stop pacing, he walked him further from the building and tried to reason with him. He made it a point to say that there is no way Mike would be allowed back in, and attempting to do so would only hurt the team. He said to think of what his parents would say and what Lucia would think. Never mind the crowd who will be watching him when, or if, he is allowed to play for the team again.

Mikell said that no one that he had known with a volatile temper ever helped himself or herself into any easy situations but just got themselves deeper into unnecessary bullshit. Mikell knew he was outside the gym for too long and he had to get back to the court, but he wasn't sure what Mike would do if he left him.

When Mike had a chance to breathe, he swore that he would not let what Asher said go. Mikell pointed out that it's just words, and Asher is big on shooting his mouth off. This wasn't enough for Mike, however, as he was determined to confront Asher the first chance he got. Mikell said he needed to get inside. He would play his ass off to make sure they won so that Mike would not be blamed for the loss.

Finally, Mike relented and said that he would head home. His parents weren't attending the game, so he would have some serious explaining to do, again. This was getting tiring. He didn't want to put this on them, and yet somehow he got himself into situations that yielded nothing but trouble. He was going straight down the same route his brother was, just using a different vehicle to get to his parents' souls.

Mike assured Mikell that he was good and he would walk off his aggravation. Mikell assessed whether he was buying it, decided he was not sure, but gave Mike the benefit of the doubt. He reminded Mike that shit would be hard, but it would work out.

"My Pops always told me that all will be good in the end. And if it's not good, then it's not the end." Mikell jerked his head up and back to signal to Mike that it was time for him to get back and that Mike should walk home. Then he headed to the gym with a head full of his own concerns, thoughts, and a suddenly growing headache.

***

Mike left his car at the court. He needed to walk home. It was a haul but he needed to burn time anyway. He could always catch a ride to get his car later, so he wasn't too worried. He didn't really trust himself behind the wheel at the moment anyway. He would need to be honest with his parents, and while he thought they would understand, he suspected his father would not exactly disagree with some of Asher's points and that turned his stomach.

It was hard enough for his dad to accept that he liked rap, but he had to set an example of some sort for his sons, and he certainly couldn't have it coming out that he had antiquated, old-school views, that he was very well aware we're not popular in the mainstream would cause the family more problems. But at this point, Mike could only think about so much.

The lengthy walk did help clear his head a bit. He walked and became keenly aware that he was having vocal conversations with himself, first sounding out what a conversation with his mother would be like, then his father, then moving on to how he was going to explain this to the coach. He found himself stressing about how the team would do without him. They were capable of winning, but he was aware that he added an element to his team that they needed and would miss on the court. Even if he was sitting off the court with a towel like Lancing deemed, at least he would be there for moral support.

By the time he got to his house, Mike had made some decisions about his conversations, explanations, and rationalizations of most things going on. He even accepted that Asher did touch upon something that was bothering him on a deep, subconscious level. He did seem to be prone to altercations and unpredictable moodiness. That day, he swore to himself that he would act with a rational mind more going forward.

As he reached his house, he noticed his father's car was not anywhere near their door, though living in Southie you could be parking miles away some days. His mother's car had not moved since this morning. Mike took a deep breath and cautiously stepped inside.

***

Mikell played great in the first half, but in the opening minutes of the second, an errant drive to the basket caused him to collide knees with the opposing team's center, and that derailed his effectiveness. Every time he attempted a crossover or a breakaway, he felt his knee begin to buckle, so he scaled back.

Running by the sidelines he could see Lancing's questioning looks, wanting to get seated, but not wanting to let the team down. The game was close already, with his team down by 3 to 5 points on a persistent basis. The most distracting thing of all was seeing Asher's face. With his team losing, every time Asher and Mikell locked eyes, Asher's face grew into a smirk. At one point, he even suddenly make an ape-like motion, pretending to scratch his armpits once, and later, subtly pounded his check, King Kong style.

Mikell already knew how he felt about Asher and didn't blame Mike for wanting to give his guy a fist or ten subsequent fists to his smug jaw. This prick was great at driving everyone absolutely up the wall. Mikell wasn't going to make Mike's mistake, but damn was he tempted to. For now, he had to put this head in the game.

In the end, Mikell got his groove back to an extent, unfortunately, the other team got theirs back harder. As the fourth quarter went on, the opponents began pulling away further, and when the final buzzer went off, they had prevailed by a 9-point margin.

***

Lancing walked off the court annoyed after the game wrapped up. He could take losing, he had coached a team that lost plenty. It was also only one game. But he was annoyed at how things went down. By no means was this a playoff shuttering dagger, but to have a kid who he pushed and vouched for, against the stigma of inciting fights, Mike painted a worse picture of the school than he had up to that point, making Lancing's efforts look like trash in the process.

In his head, he knew he had to get Mike back on the floor to have any chance against the upcoming teams that were going to be a hell of a lot harder to handle, nevermind if they made the playoffs, but he staked his reputation on his recruitment efforts, and he was not going to have his integrity compromised by some hotheads.

On his way home after the game, Lancing seriously debated what he should do, and how he would approach handling the situation with Mike.

***

Mike took the rest of Saturday and Sunday to do little of anything. He laid down and watched movies, played on his phone, and got his weekend homework done. It was nice to pull away from his normally busy life. He was honest with his parents, but it didn't lessen their concern that one of their sons was lost to the world of drugs, while the other now seemed to have a consistent propensity for ending up in fights.

He didn't feel that this was actually true, but he couldn't argue that between the BNBL, the train, and the altercation with Asher, an outside observer could think that he actually did have that problem. He was also mixed in his feelings about Lucia's decision-making. She texted him multiple times, and he ignored the texts figuring he would answer her when he was less mad.

Unfortunately, the waiting made Lucia think he didn't want to talk to her. When Mike finally reached out, she seemed relieved but did say that her mom had heard about the fight on the train and asked her if she was anywhere around there. Lucia hesitantly lied and said she was not. Mike guessed she didn't think her mother would ever come across the video online.

Mike may have been a little bit too forceful in questioning how people would know he was on stage. Lucia was caught off guard because she thought that posting it was a great thing to show the world, but Mike was tunnel-visioned on only the fact that Asher had seen it, and threw it in his face. The conversation between Mike and Lucia, therefore, left off in an awkward place.

Going to sleep on Sunday night, Mike realized that in just two days, from experiencing an amazing stage appearance with Sleepy Hollow and making a more solid friend of Mikell, some internal demons of his were pushing people he cared about away and forcing himself into a tough predicament. Perhaps he was due for a little soul searching.

Maybe if he took a more rational approach to things, he could work to improve his situation in the various screwed-up segments of his life. Perhaps if he kept focused on the important things and purged listening to crap spew from the mouth of Asher, and, as he suspected, some of his neighborhood friends, he would be better off.

He closed his eyes deciding that he would handle things more maturely going forward. With the right attitude, things would surely get better. Unfortunately, more stress and pressure were looming on the horizon...

Chapter 22

Lancing was able to smooth over Mike's situation with the school heads after the game. The school politics were a bit lighter to manipulate since the principal was looking to have a winning basketball team or at least a top-notch contender. Therefore, principal McAlluife had to look tough while still allowing for the possibility of being a contender.

The week following his outburst, Lancing saw Mike in his office and explained that there were conditions to his reinstatement. He had time to be better informed about what happened and had a separate meeting with Asher who left the meeting with a huff. He was already an alternate, and now he was threatened with expulsion from the team.

Lancing forced both Mike and Asher to go into the locker room, stand up, and issue an apology in front of the team before a practice, which Mike was not yet allowed to participate in. He made it clear that neither was blamed for the previous game's loss, but the eyes of the community and the local papers have gotten wind of all the events (though lighter on some facts than others). Mike had to swallow his desire to put Asher on blast for the things he said, and Asher issued a half-assed apology mostly centered on inciting Mike's rage when he was in an "emotionally fragile state."

Mike bit his lips through this facade and pushed on, telling the team that he had a rough night before the game where he was attacked, though he suspected the guys saw it happen. He tried to leave Mikell out of the conversation, though it was pretty clear that he was involved too.

To his credit, Mikell pulled Mike aside and offered to speak up to Lancing and the other coaches, but Mike said that there was no reason for both of them to be going through what he was enduring, and told Mikell it was a better idea if he kept to himself as much as possible with this situation. Mikell decided that he would oblige until an opportunity came up to talk to Lancing himself.

After the apologies were issued, Lancing informed Mike that if his bruises had healed enough and he could have the team's trainer evaluate his physical standing the day before the next game, Mike would be allowed to play in it. Mike was psyched to hear this but he had his mind on other matters.

For one thing, things at home were getting tough. His brother, more bitter than ever about being forced into rehabilitation, outright refused any contact from Mike's parents. While there was a seeming upswing, the desire to get back to being high was far too great. Mike wasn't sure if he was now too far gone for recovery. His mom cried daily about it, while his father, stoic to a fault in the matter, was yielding hints of being extremely bothered by the whole situation.

For Mike personally, the video Lucia posted drew the attention of other students, who were more of Asher's state of mind. Asher himself proved to be an insincere scumbag as he would find ways, on the daily, to give Mike shit about rapping at the show. He wouldn't get it through his head that Mike actually had a great time with that, leaving all the problems of the world elsewhere, while he was able to live out a surreal experience. The sheer volume of biting comments from Asher and friends though, made Mike second guess whether he should have gone on that stage or not.

Of course, this was mostly known because Lucia, in an ill-fated attempt to show how proud she was of her new possible boyfriend, not only posted the video of Mike and Mikell on stage with Sleepy but actively showed it to her friends too. She even smoothed things over with her mother on the topic of Mike.

Too bad Mike was in a bad mental state and he let the nagging and bullying get to him. Sure, it wasn't physical, but the constant jabs at his actions started to make him question his decision and, worse than that, question whether he trusted Lucia or her judgment. He didn't want to think about it, but the stress forced it on him.

This strained his relationship with her. He was more distant and seemed to brush her off in a manner that bordered on rudeness. Lucia was insightful enough that she sensed what was going on, which made her feel incredibly guilty. She even tried to talk to Mike on the way out of school one day, but he made up an excuse about needing to help his mom and took off before much of a conversation happened.

***

Mikell had an easier time at school, though he witnessed Mike putting up with a lot of shit from Asher and others, so he wanted to intervene, even though Mike specifically asked him to stay out of it. Mikell did have a plan in mind. He would go talk to Lancing himself. However, he considered how this would look to Mike, and held his tongue on the matter, briefly. Ultimately, Lancing asked to talk to him, and Mikell went in and said his piece.

Where Mikell would face a bit more issues was at home. Pops was a smart man and picked up on Mikell being distant and lost in his own world. It wasn't long before he went for a cut at his favorite barbershop, and was told by the other men that his son was in a fight. Mikell hid his bruises well enough till they healed, but he couldn't control others speaking up to Pops whether he was around or not.

Pops grilled him on the events of that night, and Mikell pleaded his case. Pops surprised him by saying that he was proud of Mikell's noble actions, but that he was an idiot for being that way when it could have taken everything he had. Mikell didn't even consider how this could have panned out for him if things had gone even a little differently. Never mind that the video was circulating about, and any viewer, depending on the angle of the shot, when the video was started and when it was cut off, as well as "creative" editing could result in it seeming like the events went quite a bit differently than they did.

The biggest concern was the fact that this may end up with the authorities who might be interested in the parties involved in the fight. They might dig deeper to find out who was involved, and Pops did not want or need his son to be in their crosshairs if they showed up looking for him. All of these concerns reminded Mikell that no good deed goes unpunished. This was not a world of right and wrong, noble and dastardly, or even a fair one. It was all about perception. Nothing one does will be universally viewed as the "right thing." He was frustrated with himself for not coming to the realization sooner.

But what's done is done now, and everyone has to move forward regardless of the fallout that comes after. So that is what Mikell decided to do. He would keep his head down and make the best decision possible at the moment, focusing on his court performance above anything. After all, this was the factor paramount to anything else to him just a few weeks ago.

***

After a week, Mike's face healed up almost entirely, and the day before the next game he showed up at Lancing's office to speak to the coach about his presence on the court the next day. After a lengthy conversation, the two agreed that Mike would be able to play, but he needed to keep a civil tongue and avoid any conflicts and indiscretions from this point going forward. The coach explained that he now saw the video and it was unclear to him who started the fight, but he did tell Mike that Mikell explained what happened.

Mike gritted his teeth as he did ask Mikell to stay out of it, but this was information that could have only come from someone who was in the midst of the situation. The huge benefit of Mikell speaking up is that Lancing knew of the past between the two better than most, and if it was Mikell who spoke up for Mike, of all people, Lancing had to treat that as a valid stance since it's not likely that Mikell would speak up for someone he couldn't stand just a few weeks back.

The ends, as it seemed, justified the means here. Mike resigned to not hold it against Mikell that he violated his request. Turns out, it only helped him. Dealing with Asher and his mouth, especially when it came to calling Lucia names is something Mike would have a harder time with. He still harbored some resentment for the video post, but he was learning to accept that she was not being careless or intending harm.

After his conversation with the coach, he spotted Lucia talking to a friend in the hallway and sheepishly approached her, hoping to mend their strained relationship. Lucia hesitantly excused herself from her conversation and walked outside the school with Mike. They talked for a while and came to an understanding. Lucia felt bad about how her action amplified Mike's situation with the team, and Mike admitted that a lot of his frustration was largely misdirected and that he realized her posting the video was coming from a good place. They parted on civil terms, though neither was quite ready for their next date just yet. After all, if the first one was any indication of how they would go, they might both be rightfully concerned.

***

Mike arrived at the school hours before the game, got changed, and went to shoot around. Except for Lancing and one of the assistant coaches, no one was even there yet. His physical evaluation went by smoothly, so he was conditionally allowed to participate again.

Only the security personnel were starting to arrive to man the doors with the people streaming in. Mike warmed up, nodding to Lancing who spotted him early on and started to run drills, taking shots at the basket. He was energized and honing his focus on the game. The practice shot success rate was only about 50%, which was concerning, he was typically a better shooter at warm-ups, but he took a mini hiatus from the game, and he only practiced once with the team the day before, and that practice largely consisted of trying to avoid eye contact with any teammates, Asher specifically.

As the team, his own and the opposing one began to arrive, the crowd of excited parents and kids began to file in as well. There was a growing hum of anticipation as more people entered the gym and it made Mike more anxious than excited about the attention. Mikell showed up shortly after and after heading to the locker room, he came out on the court for warm-ups as well. The refs gathered up the coaches and were discussing something off to the side, so Mikell approached Mike.

"You good?" - he tried to ask subtly.

Mike cast a suspicious glance around the gym. "I've been better....but worse too. Listen, I know I said to keep out of things and let me handle this one, but I do appreciate you speaking up about what happened to Lancing."

"Yeah, I figured that would get back to you. The last game was a good lesson that this team needs you on the court. And here you are so I guess it was worth it." - Mikell replied.

Mike nodded. "Let's get back in it today then."

"Fuck yeah" - Mikell replied with a smile.

Chapter 23

The rust from lack of mutual practices was evident throughout the first quarter of the game. Mike thought back to the shootaround and his lackluster shooting percentage and felt a bit deflated. Lancing allowed Mike to start the game, but when the performance was lacking with only a breakaway layup being Mike's only successful bucket in nearly 4 minutes, Lancing sat him to try to get back up on the board.

Mikell was having a very good game, pouring in 8 points in the same time period. Lancing kept him in the game longer but ultimately sat him just over 6 minutes in for the sake of preserving the energy the team needed. The rest of the team held their own, showing that even with their two-star players out of the game, they could stay competitive. Patesh drained a couple of sorely needed threes to keep the team afloat.

Mike sipped his water and watched the back and forth on the court, cheering for his team's successes. He couldn't help but cast a side-eye to the end of the bench, where Asher sat quietly, very obviously stewing in his personal misery of still being a deep bench alternate. Every time Asher turned his eyes to Mike, Mike turned his gaze either back to the court or the crowd. He was trying to see if Lucia was anywhere in sight, and while she may have been in attendance, he had yet to spot her.

He tried to keep focused on the game. After the last couple of weeks, finally getting back on the court was a privilege he didn't want to waste. When the buzzer went off ending the game's first quarter, the team huddled together to get some instructions from Lancing. They were staying in the game, but just barely, being down by 8 points. The opposing team would have possession at the start of the second quarter.

***

Mikell found himself panting on the bench. He was playing harder than ever in this game and his energy was sapped. Was he coming down with something? What a shit time for that to happen...not that there is ever a good time. He pounded his drink and watched the court. The quarter came to a close, and Lancing instructed him to stay on the bench. Mikell wondered if Lancing sensed something was off with him already.

Mikell stretched his legs out and pulled them back hoping to generate some kind of "spring" into them. He felt little change in terms of energy. Growing concerned he tried to calm himself with deep, slow breaths. Something was going on...like a nagging feeling he couldn't shake.

The first half got on the way and the team was doing better, but still lagging. Every time they pulled within 5 points, the opponents would sink a jumper or a three, then force a turnover, and get another score. This was a cycle that kept repeating. Mike grew anxious to get back in the game and kept glancing over at the coach for a sign that he wanted to get in. Lancing was not looking back, focusing on the court, shouting instructions, and calling plays.

Mike noticed that his team was falling into a zone defense, a strategy typical of a team with deficient defensive capabilities. He tapped his foot looking around. Once his eyes turned to the far end of the court, he caught Asher glaring at him. The two locked eyes. A sick smile drew across Asher's face and a chuckle that was not audible due to the noise of the gym, but visibly obvious to an observer escaped.

Mike didn't like that one bit. He knew Asher was a racist, disingenuous prick, but he had hoped that he was all talk. Something about that smile told him Asher had more in mind. Mike couldn't think about this. He turned his attention, only to realize the Lancing was calling him. When he turned, Lancing said: "Jesus kid, wake up! Be present! Get in. You're on number 5."

Mike threw down his towel and quickly headed to the scorer's table to check in, passing by Asher, not looking in his direction. He entered the game with new energy, a nervous one, but a powerful one nonetheless. He turned to enter the court, only to realize Lancing had sent Mikell in too. If there was ever a time to apply his efforts, this was it.

The ball was inbounded and Mike got on man-to-man defense against the bushy-haired kid with the number 5 jersey. He was determined to stick to him like flies to fresh crap, but the kid proved very elusive. Mike refocused his game. A couple of possession changes in, and number 5 ended up with the ball, which Mike became hyper-focused on. His efforts weren't fruitless, as he managed to knock the ball loose from the kid's hand and attempt a breakaway, but the defenders caught up and got in his way.

From the corner of his eyes, Mike spotted James, the team's backup point guard, so Mike whipped him the ball, and James swung it to the quickly approaching Mikell who drove into the paint for an outrageously aggressive dunk. This made the gym pop intensely and Mike felt a stir in his heart. The excitement was coming back to the game. He hung back a moment to slap Mikell's hand as he ran by, and then turned just to notice Lucia on her feet cheering her heart out.

The half was nearly over and things were certainly looking up. The team took a two-point lead and was able to stave off the opposition, holding them to that lead as the buzzer went off for the half. The excitement for this game was palpable. The next two games would be away so it was enthralling to have the crowd be going this nuts for them. The team headed off to the locker room, with Lancing in tow. He wasn't smiling. Then again he never seemed to be.

***

The team entered the locker room, blasting with excitement, slapping the lockers, and high-fiving each other. Even Mikell, typically, a subdued guy, was distributing compliments and smiles. Lancing came in and clapped his hands.

"Glad to see some life out there gentlemen. Looks like we are turning this ship around. I'm gonna level with you though, you are better players than those guys..." - cheers erupted from most of the guys and someone threw out a "hell yeah!" to which Lancing raised his hands to quiet the crew. "...but, a blind man could see that they are much faster than you. Sometimes I look at you guys on that court and I think I'm watching a herd of tortoises, stampeding through peanut butter. You were never the Usain Bolts of the world, but today you are groggy as shit out there. Whatever it is that is slowing you down, eliminate it, and do so as quickly as possible. We are up by two, and if I'm grading your performance on a curve, it isn't looking like a top-ranked scoring squad here. You guys are up by sheer luck right now. While you are over here celebrating your halftime victories, the game isn't over for another half, so let's get our shit together, head into the game, and pick up the pace. Let's see some hustle in the next go-around."

"Way to be a downer coach..." - someone said from the back of the locker room.

"You said realist wrong, son." - replied Lancing in a snarky tone.

The boys were quieter now, all heading to their lockers for towels and sitting down for a drink of water. Mike went to open his locker to check his phone. He knew it wasn't the time or place but he was secretly hoping Lucia had texted him. Seeing her in the crowd was encouraging. Lancing stretched in the aisle right next to him.

Mike swung open the locker door and caught his jacket nearly hitting the ground, clearly falling off his hanger. He grabbed it mid-air, replaced by his catlike reflexes. Lancing turned to see what the noise was, only to see Mike picking the jacket back up to put in his locker. Mike wasn't going to be sneaking a check on his phone now he guessed.

He looked at Lancing with a half-smile as if to acknowledge his clumsiness, but the coach was looking down at the floor. Mike was confused but put the jacket back as Lancing bent down to the floor. He picked something up off the ground and brought it to his face. His eyes darted at Mike. Lancing was holding a bag of colorful pills in his hand.

With a glare borne of pure betrayal, Lancing's stare was burning a hole through Mike's face. Mike, confused, looked closer, and he instinctually reached for the bag to bring it closer to his face. Lancing yanked it away. "Is this what I fucking think it is??" - Lancing growled under his breath.

The rest of the team stopped what they were doing and turned to the coach. "I don't know, what ....what is that? Wait, coach, are you saying...? Nah, that shit is not mine, I don't even know what that is." - Mike started

"Pretty sure no one knows what's in Molly. Except for meth, Mike. Meth...and a bunch of other shit I can't name. And you thought it would be a good idea to bring this here?"

"Coach ...wait...."- Mike tried to speak again, looking around at the staring faces in the crowd.

"No! Sit your ass on that bench and do not move until the game is over, then, you and I are gonna talk....alone!" - he raised his voice and looked over his shoulder as the other boys quickly lowered their eyes.

"Coach, I don't know what that crap is, but it isn't mine. I'm telling you..." - Mike tried again.

"After. The. Game. Is. OVER! If you are not sitting in that exact spot when I come back after the game, I will not due you the courtesy of hearing you out." - Lancing snapped. He then got close to Mike and said in an audible grumble: "You not being here means I call the cops first, and they will talk with you instead of me. Sit your ass down!"

The sweat from the game was nothing compared to how hard Mike was sweating now. A million thoughts ran through his head, all confusion. He didn't want to look at the other players' faces. He was embarrassed, yet why should he be, whatever that was, he knew it wasn't his.

Lancing waved everyone off out of the locker room and pointed to Mike with the angriest of looks. A couple of guys questioned why they had to head back out so early in halftime, to which Lancing snapped at them to go warm up. He pointed to the seat and nodded his head before following the team out. Mike put his head in his hands. The locker room quieted and his nervous ticks began to overtake him. He started tapping the floor with his feet and scratching his head from front to back. The stress and tension were too much. Then....someone spoke, making Mike jerk his head right up.

"Guess you can't get on stage at a CRAP show and leave backstage without little girl Molly on your arm ha?" - Mike glared up to see Asher, wiping his hands with a paper towel just coming out of the bathroom. "Throwin your future away kid..." - he said, his voice dripping with sarcasm.

Mike got up but remembered Lancing's warning, so he stood in place staring at Asher. Asher finished up with the paper towel, crumbled it up, and tossed it on the ground next to Mike. "For the tears..."

"You little mother fu...." - but Asher was already out of the locker room door. Mike was left standing there, befuddled, furious, and ready to chase Asher down. It must have been that little shit, he thought. The smirk earlier made sense now.

***

On the court, the team was out of sorts. What they just witnessed in the locker room shook them to their core. Mikell didn't know Mike but got the feeling it was not in his nature to go the party drug style.

Maybe he'd sneak some liquor or pot, but no way was he capable of chancing it during basketball. If there was one thing he knew, it was that Mike would not actively jeopardize his playing. Part of Mikell told him Mike was a lot like him in a way. Wouldn't sacrifice this opportunity for something stupid. Though Mikell had to admit, he did get into a fight on the train, and that was pretty dumb and risky.

He glanced back at the locker room, just in time to see a smirking Asher make his way out and head to the bench. Mikell's wheels started to turn.

The second half was weird. The crowd certainly noticed that Mike Cassidy wasn't on the court or even on the bench. Murmurs traveled around. Lucia sat looking concerned. She did her best to try to get Mikell's attention when he was near. He was busy concentrating on the game, but at one point he happened to look in her direction. She opened her eyes wide and glared questionably at him. He subtly shook his head from side to side. Lucia sat down. She didn't know what that meant. But it was obvious that it wasn't good.

Mike heard the crowd outside, the screeching of sneakers, and the outbursts of excitement. But it all became background noise. The time he had to sit and think of what to do next should have had his mind running about his upcoming conversation with Lancing. His future on the team and the school.

But all Mike could think about is whether his parents would believe the bullshit that he is going through. They have been too busy to attend most of the games, so it was certainly for the best that they weren't there that day. But between his fight on the train and the situation with his brother, this news would most certainly break them. He had kept Eddie's addiction, rehab, and the painful family dynamic to himself and didn't share it with anyone at school. If only they knew what he had lived through and how hard his life experiences pushed him from even ever thinking of touching drugs.

Molly, though? Who gets Molly? With the legalization of weed and the almost normalization of high school-age drinking, these are things that are expected. Molly was on another level. Anyone in possession of that amount of Molly was not intending to use the drug. They intended to sell it.

His locker wasn't locked, but he also didn't have anything except his phone, car keys, and wallet which were about as prized of possessions, and little chance anyone from the team would go in to steal anything. Too stupid.

Therefore, if no one believed him, he would be viewed as a kid who intended to distribute the drug with a seriously high hospitalization and fatality rate in the school. And Asher, fucking Asher, with his comment, he was in the bathroom when it went down, but he knew what Mike was found to have on him. What other explanation could there be outside of Asher being behind this?

Asher was definitely responsible, but it was Mike's word against his, and the two already had beef, so of course, he would accuse him. Problem is, he had no proof. He was a framed man who was about to suffer persecution and consequences for something he had no way of disproving.

The night of the concert floated through his mind again. While the memories were largely positive, they did make him think of all the people in the community who came to that show. It made him think of Mikell too, and the lingering thoughts of the hardships of persecution against his community that people had to endure. It turned Mike's stomach.

Mike resolved that he would fight this and overcome the burden of proof that was not put upon him, but hard as he might think about it, he did not think of a way out of this one. He would fight it nonetheless.

The final buzzer shook him from his daze. Now it was only a matter of time until he was going to have to face the music. He didn't bother showering. Acting quickly, he yanked off his jersey, wiping his body with it, then the sweat off his head. He quickly threw his locker open again and grabbed a long-sleeved shirt he meant to wear after the game. He then changed out of his pants. As he was buckling his belt, the locker room door opened, and the team, dejected from another close loss, walked in. Mike sat on the same part of the bench, looking down, holding his jersey in his hands.

Chapter 24

Try as he might, Mike was unable to convince Lancing of his innocence. It wasn't that Lancing didn't want to hear him, it was the fact he couldn't let this go. He was not aware of Mike's life experiences and how drugs have wrecked his family. He could not fathom the pain that this would cause Mike's parents. Mike hoped they wouldn't believe it, that he would never subject them to the things his brother did, but even the thought that now this was a possibility would linger, and it would be a torrent of stress and sadness on their souls.

Mike let Lancing speak his piece in his office, then he formally stated that the drugs were not his, and he wouldn't even know how to go about getting them. But he wanted to honestly tell the coach that he strongly suspect Asher, though he had no proof. Even if he made the accusation all Asher had to do was deny saying anything and that avenue would be cut off.

Mike felt desperate. He had managed to climb out of every hole he put himself into over the last few weeks. Now, he was lucky to escape with anything short of the cops being involved. Lancing told Mike outright that he could not simply look the other way even if he did believe him. Hell, the entire team saw the bag of Molly.

It could not be swept under the rug regardless. Mike gritted his teeth to not remind Lancing that it was he who saw the bag and said something about it, so he is really the reason the team knew.

The conversation ended with Lancing telling Mike that he was not only suspended from the team, but he would need to go up the chain. If he didn't, someone from the team would, and then Lancing's ass was grass. He recognized how unfair that was, but he had a mortgage, kids in college, and lots of bills. If he got banned from coaching basketball here under these circumstances, no school in the lower 48 would take him. He'd lose his house, wife, and respectability. For him, there was no second-guessing.

He told Mike to go straight home and to tell his parents about this before they got a call. The best he could do was to give Mike until the next school day before he spoke to the principal. Mike held his head down, defeated, and slowly shuffled to the door.

"Kid...." - Lancing said in a softer tone. "If you have proof, tangible, actual, indisputable proof of this not being yours, you best bring it up soon. Very soon. I believe you, but this is a situation with no escape clause for either of us. I am not asking you to fall on your sword but the mistakes you have made so far, and now this... it's catching up. I hope you think of something. I want you to be vindicated."

Mike thought it was a nice gesture but also cruel to give him hope like that. Mike never looked back, simply exiting the office and shuffling down the hall, pulling a hood over his head to keep the direct eye contact with anyone he passed by to an absolute minimum.

**

Mikell stood outside the doors of the school looking around. He saw Mike come out of the door and caught up to him.

"Yo...wait up. What'd coach say?" - Mikell asked, walking alongside Mike.

After a moment of silence, Mike replied. "You're the star of the squad now. Alone and shiny. So if you want to do something with the season, this is your time to do it."

Mikell put his arm on Mike's shoulder and stopped him. Mike never looked up. "He booted you from the team? You told him that shit wasn't yours, he didn't believe you??"

"Pretty sure he believed every word, but the whole team saw it, and if he hides this, it's full ruin for him. Even if he was to speak up for me, the prick who planted those will just contradict it and ruin everyone's standing anyway so, he didn't have much of a choice."- Mike answered.

"Wait, hold up. Do you know who planted them in your locker? Who the fuck would do that...oh.." - a lightbulb went off. "You know it was that little racist bitch, Asher?"

"He basically admitted it so, yeah man, it was him. No doubt. Where he got a bag like that, I have no fucking clue, but I don't really care. I'm off the team, gonna get booted from the school I'm sure next week, and now I get to go home and tell my parents that their other child is an accused junkie too...." - he stopped himself.

Mikell didn't question this. It didn't seem like the sort of thing he would want to get into. "Why not force Asher to admit it? Out his ass."

"Come on man....get fucking real." - Mike ripped down his hood and looked at Mikell. "This ain't no cop show. I'm not a detective, questioning a perp. He will never admit to it. Listen, just do me a favor, make sure that you are never in a position to be off the team, and do your best to help everyone else advance so that that little prick has to ride the bench."

"Don't worry about the court shit, Mike. Listen, my boys would say that you are a white boy with white boy problems. And you are. But, you're my white boy, and you're on my team. So you don't do anything stupid. I'll see what I can do about that little bitch." - Mikell said

"You don't need to do shit for me. We had an alliance of coincidence, maybe more than once. I appreciate you having my back on the train and now, but this is not something that we can maneuver out of. So let's stop pretending that we can. You go lead that team to the best rest of the season you can." - Mike pulled his hood back up and bolted. Mikell looked after him. Then he walked to get to his bus. He would need time to think.

***

Laying with his face buried in the pillow, Mike was ready to scream. He had come home and sat his parents down after dinner the night of the game, and explained to them what happened. He swore up and down that the Molly wasn't his but he had no way to prove it. He begged that his parents would not reach out to the school as they would be reaching out to them before long, of that he was certain.

Did they believe him? After several hours, he thought so, but it didn't mean that it didn't hit them hard and deep. He was open about a conflict with another kid on the team, something he managed to keep under wraps since the time it happened by sheer luck. He described Asher as being an utter lowlife who was only friends with him before he realized Mike was into things commonly associated with African American culture.

His father did interject and ask why exactly he was into that stuff after all, which made Mike regret bringing up the topic. He knew his father was an old-school mindset, and he knew those were hard to break after years of affirmation on one's mind. Oddly, Mike understood the pressures of society to push certain antiquated beliefs on people, keeping the unnecessary divide going forward. Mike suspected that if he didn't get into rap, he might have ended up in the same camp. Rap pulled him into that culture, and immersion is an eye-opening teacher for certain.

In any case, the conversation did bring his mother to tears, multiple times. Mike hated Asher already, but this made Asher's existence a reality Mike could not stand. It took everything he had to suppress his rage and keep his composure. And that he did on a minimal scale.

The following Monday, his parents did in fact receive a call requesting a meeting with the coach and the principal. Mike was banned from the team while an investigation was pending, and he was to have no presence at any of the games even as a spectator. McAullife was dead set on calling the cops, but Lancing did go to bat for Mike, saying that not only did he already dispose of the Molly after the game (claiming to not have been thinking) but also personally found Mike's pleas of innocence credible. He knew the latter would never be enough to sway McAullife, but the former did tie his hands to an extent. This helped Mike escape suspension and expulsion from the school, which he was thankful for. But if he wasn't going to play ball here, what was the point?

Asher floated around the school halls with his newfound crew of like-minded pricks like he was surfing on cloud nine. Mike wanted very badly to confront him but knew that he was in a hole deep enough that he did not need to pick up that shovel.

On Wednesday morning Mike's mother came in to sit with the coach and the principal. Mike's father couldn't get out of work, and Mike thought it was for the best. He wasn't sure how his father would deal with the situation. The discussion quickly brought Mike's mother to tears and not because she assumed Mike's guilt, but because of the raw nerve that it hit with her other son on the topic. Both the coach and the principal were caught entirely off-guard by the topic of Mike's brother being an addict in rehab. Mike was pulled from his morning classes to come in while his mom tried to stand strong and explain why this accusation can never be true due to family issues.

The regret in Lancing's eyes during the discussion was obvious, but he held firm in that this was the right process. He did interject and try to ask that Mike not be removed entirely from the team and that he still got to practice with them at least on a probationary basis. McAullife saw this as a way to make an example for anyone else in the school who wanted to bring in drugs, and that was nearly more important to him than keeping a star player on the team. He would only go as far as to permit Mike to be at the practices in order to observe and listen to the coaching and strategizing, but not on the court. Lancing would take what he could get.

***

Three weeks came and went, as Mike sat on the sidelines and was prevented from attending the games. The first of those games still found the team reeling and readjusting, though Mikell tried his best to step up his game, the team managed to blow a small lead and lose once again. The playoff hopes were growing grim at the beginning of the season. But in the second of the three, the frustrated team came out firing on all cylinders, determined not to allow another game to get blown. This time, the squad eked out a 3-point victory. The excitement was a bit subdued, however. They were still in the red in terms of win/loss records.

The third game was some type of blessing, though Lancing didn't see it that way. They played a team that was already considered one of the weakest in the division, plus their best player hurt his shoulder and was out for several weeks. Mikell and the team blew this team away with a stunning 19-point crush of a win, but the celebration was cut short by Lancing's sharp speech to the team after the game.

This was not one that they should be proud of. This was hardly competition. A weak team with an injured player. Beating them was like winning a race against a sloth and being proud of it. This was not the standard they wanted to measure themselves against. The guys didn't like the downer-coach behavior, but they really couldn't argue with his perspective.

Asher made it a point to ask every week to be back in the lineup, sometimes multiple times. Lancing, suspicious of him already, yet not having any evidence to levy an accusation, kept saying he will think about it. After the third game, the guys went out to grab a pizza to celebrate the win, but Mikell hung back, saying that he had to get back home to help Pops with something that day. As he headed out of the locker room, he overheard a conversation around the corner. It was Asher talking to two of his buddies. Mikell's ears perked up and he stopped short behind the corner, entirely obstructed by lockers to listen. He would have to walk past them to leave and he really didn't want to bother doing so.

"...not that I know of. Anyway, no one even knows about that shit." - Mikell heard Asher say.

"You're playing with fire here man. Any school values their basketball team and their wins way more than busting a player for drugs. I mean that kid got into a brawl on the T, and they let him come back in two weeks. And that Mkell kid, he was in it too, and no one even lifted a finger. Probably afraid of accusations from the fucking woke-ass parents." - said another kid.

"Holy shit!" thought Mikell. He had taken the phone out of his pocket and was quickly searching for the microphone app.

"You taking a hard chance Ash, if they fingerprint that bag ...."

"Three weeks later? Get real." - Asher spat back.

Mikell found the app opened it and tapped the microphone to activate it.

"You don't know if they called the cops about it or not though" - said the third kid.

"If they were gonna do that, they would have done it already. Lancing is just a bitch like the rest of them, trying to save face and save his job at the same time. It's been nearly a month, and that little scapegoat Cassidy hasn't even been allowed in the building for games. He is dealt with, they have no way to prove shit. And at this point, no one is gonna bother. Well worth the money I ponied up for the Molly."

Mikell couldn't help but smirk and shake his head. "Keep digging asshole." - he thought.

"At least you wouldn't get your knee caps broken for not paying that shit back in time. Good to have a cousin in the trade, ha?" - said the first kid.

"Yeah yeah, keep it down, this is the last time we talk about this shit here. Let's go." - Asher said.

"You going to go with your team" - asked one of the kids.

"Fuck them! They shoved me to the deep bench when they brought in blackie and wanna-be blackface. They ain't my team anymore. They are all pussies anyways, including Lancing. Hope some of them choke on their fucking pizzas." - Asher snapped. He then quieted his voice. "Let's go.."

Mikell tapped the microphone again. He listened for Asher and his friends to walk off, tapped his phone against his chin, and smiled. He turned and headed for another exit out of the school, quietly singing under his breath: "Bad boys, bad boys, whatcha gonna do, whatcha gonna do when they come for you...."

Chapter 25

After practice the following week, the guys on the team were changing in the locker room when Lancing came in to discuss their upcoming matchup. The team they were playing this weekend was the runner-up to the championship last year in their division and Lancing wanted to make sure that everyone knew their delineated roles. He told the team that they need to stop living on the hype of their accomplishment from last week, beating a weaker, depleted team was not something to be celebrated.

At this point, they would need to be focused on every single game as if it was the team's last, or they would find themselves mathematically eliminated from playoff contention. This season was supposed to be their big shake-up, so getting ousted from the playoffs was not something they could afford. Lancing told the team to taper their expectations about how far they'd go and to not think too far ahead. Every game mattered at this point. No more throwaways.

Mike sat on the far end of the bench separate from the team with his hoodie over his head. He was told not to interact with people if he didn't have to. He was present but was otherwise regarded as a non-entity in the locker room until his name would be cleared. Asher on the other hand took this as an opportunity to do some sucking up to the coach and try to get back into the lineup. When the coach wrapped speaking, Asher got up and turned to the team.

"Guys, listen. I know I'm riding the bench, but I am as much a part of this team as you. No matter what I'm doing, playing or not, I am with you to the end. But let's not have it be the end. Coach is right, we gotta play every game like it's the last. We got a great thing going here, we got some good players on the squad this year, and even though one of them is not on the court with us, let's win this one and every one of the next games for Mike Cassidy." - Asher said, trying hard to sound genuine.

Mike raised his head in surprise. "Mike was a good utility guy to get us to get some wins early this season, and he is a hell of a baller. Give him a hand guys, come on." - Asher continued.

Someone shouted: "Man, shut up. Leave him alone. He got enough going on."

A couple of other players echoed the sentiment.

"Hey! HEY!" - came a booming voice from the back. The team turned to see Mikell standing up. "The man is trying to give credit to a teammate who can't join us. Let the man speak. Go ahead man" - he nodded toward

Asher gesturing him to continue. The look on Asher's face was a confluence of surprise and anxiety, sprinkled with a healthy helping of confusion. Mikell reached for his bag as he sat back down. He looked over to Mike who was glaring at him looking both confused and betrayed. In the dim lighting of the locker room, the attention focused back on Asher, at the front of the squad, Mike thought he saw Mikell wink at him.

".....Uhh....yeah, I mean, thanks .....man, that's true....we give Mike all the props. You've all seen it, the kid is a fighter....and a showman. So let's give him a hand. Come on!" Everyone hesitantly clapped and looked over at a very confused Mike. The applause filled the locker room. Mike, the coach, and Mikell were the only ones not clapping.

".... gonna do that, they would have done it already.:" - Asher's voice spoke again. The locker room quieted down and turned back to him. Asher glared stupidly to the back of the locker room. Then he spoke again, but while his voice was speaking, his mouth was mostly dropped open in genuine surprise. His voice was coming from the back of the locker room. "...Lancing is just a bitch like the rest of them, trying to save face and save his job at the same time. It's been nearly a month, and that little scapegoat Cassidy hasn't even been allowed in the building for games. He is dealt with, they have no way to prove shit. And at this point, no one is gonna bother. Well worth the money I ponied up for the Molly."

Mikell sat in the back and tapped something with his thumb. Then he looked up right at Asher. "That's some riveting shit man. Don't stop now. Go on...." He then raised his phone out of his bag and wiggled it in the air, with the cockiest smirk on his face. He glanced over to Mike who had a shit-eating grin all over his face.

Asher stood there, embarrassed, stunned, and growing redder than a beet. Lancing rose from his chair. Asher looked over at him, then at Mike, then at Mikell. Like a crazed jaguar, he leaped on the bench in front of him and dove in Mikell's direction. "Fucking darkie ass bitch, I'm fuckin kill yo ape ass!"

His impressive leap caught people off guard but by the time he was mid-jump bolting toward Mikell ready to tear him apart, the team realized what was happening and snatched him in the air, stopping his leap short, and dragging him back down. Asher swung violently, punching James in the ear, sending him reeling to the side. The other guys grabbed him around the shoulders and the waist, and Patesh grabbed at his foot relentlessly, only to have Asher's sneaker pop off. They were doing their best to restrain him from getting to Mikell or hitting anyone else. "Should've stayed in Dorchester you mother fucker, you're dead. You're dead! You won't see another morning you fucking tar baby!" - Asher was flailing violently as the team pushed him back, over the benches. They pressed him up against the lockers.

Mikell picked up his phone again and tapped the screen, the phone played again. "You're dead! You won't see another morning you fucking tar baby!" He tapped it again. "Like I said...don't stop now. Go on!"

In a flash of realization, it occurred to Asher what he was saying and what he was doing. He was too far in now to do anything about it. He was not going to let being outed and humiliated like this go unanswered. Mikell didn't move. Asher grew furious and kicked one of the boys holding him back right in the groin. The poor kid went down like a sack, while the surprised teammates relented as he shoved his thumb at one of the boy's eyes, giving him a deep cut from his upper cheek down to his mouth. In an instant, the boy grabbed at his face and Asher broke free of the grip.

He bolted right Mikell, going over the front bench, aiming straight for Mikell's face. At this point, Mikell dropped the phone back in his bag anticipating the attack. Asher hopped on the second bench as the rest of the boys were trying to get to him. He was on the third bench now, the next leap was at Mikell. Before anyone knew what happened, Asher was leaping towards him.

Something whizzed past Mkell's eyes. There was a sudden and unexpected thud that made Mikell step back, but he was left untouched as Asher's trajectory suddenly changed and he fell to the right, slamming into the lockers next to Mikell. Something had hit him right in the head, mid-leap. When Asher went down, the team's center go to him and put a knee on his back to keep him down.

In the craziness of the moment, Mikell took a second to realize that what knocked Asher off his leap was a basketball right to the side of his head. He shot a look in the direction to see where the ball came from.

Mike stood at the side alone. "Oops! I interacted. I must be really fucked now!" - he said dripping with sarcasm.

Mikell couldn't hold back a laugh. Lancing had made his way over to Asher at this point and knelt next to him. "Damn, that was a hell of a slip off that bench. If you weren't so clumsy you could have hurt someone real bad. We could go with the real story right guys?" - he looked up at the team. "But I guess I'm too much of a bitch, to tell the truth, and so are the rest of you."

Smiles popped everywhere in the locker room. Even the bleeding boy had to snicker.

"Mikell, be a gentleman and call Mr. Asher a private escort to the police station would ya?"

Mikell quickly reached for his phone and dialed 911. When he connected with a contact a moment later he said: "Yeah....we need help, there is a kid here attacking people randomly." He paused and continued. "Yeah, he is crazy. I think he might be trippin. Kept saying he is into Molly, I guess his cousin sells it to him or something."

Chapter 26

"Who would have thought that back when you two were in the middle of the city's worst riot in some time, you'd be brought together like this? Putting you two on the same team could have gone very poorly but it took an ass whooping and a foiled plan at disparaging one of you to bring you together. And I suppose your little on-stage duet helped too. The point is, you two have been through a lot in just a short while, and you have pushed through it, reluctantly at first, but you did it. I know I didn't help matters in making your lives easier, but I'm your coach, and while I'm never looking to punish the innocent, teaching tough lessons, even by accident is sort of part of the gig. And speaking of that, we got some winning to do. As in, if we don't, your first season with the squad will be a wash. Not blaming you for that one...at least not yet. We are not out just yet, and we can still push through to the playoffs, but its going to be like rolling a boulder up a vertical hill. So let's get it done. That said, I am proud of the two of you." - Lancing said.

Mike and Mikell nodded and rose from their chairs in Lancing's office. This was easily sincere and from the heart conversation that Lancing had with them since they first met him. Certainly the first time he sat them down for a chat. They nodded their appreciation and stood up and headed back out to practice.

***

Mike was reinstated to the team's active roster shortly after the incident with Asher. He had a plan that he was going to make everyone involved in his suspension feel enormously guilty for having put him through it, as he had no power to do much else. He wanted back on the team, but he wanted Lancing, McAullife, and the other assistant coaches to feel like crap for what he and his parents were put through.

It was Lucia who invited Mike to lunch and discussed the matter with him. Normally reserved about personal matters, Mike felt that after the tension with Lucia over the concert video, he owed her, of all people some openness. Lucia asked Mike to consider how this would impact his relationship with the team, his coach, and the school going forward if he made sure that they all felt his rage over these matters. Would Mike feel personally vindicated? Perhaps, but would it be worth the abrasive relationship that followed?

Besides, the people involved clearly felt guilty enough. McAullife personally apologized to Mike for the hassles and even called Mike's mother to personally apologize for putting her through something so personally rough. Lancing placed a similar phone call.

Lucia's reasoning was one that Mike didn't want to accept, but couldn't help but to do anyway. Not because he wanted to keep seeing her, but because as much as he hated to admit it, she was completely right. He would have to eat his anger and take the good things that were coming his way. His hard play on the court would help the team, and that would help the school. As the school ascended, it would help the community, not just locally but of the students involved from various districts in it. As Mike's father always said: "A rising tide lifts all ships."

***

Asher was not only taken off in handcuffs from his lockerroom outburst, he allowed himself to completely forego his right to remain silent and screamed more about his plan to take Mike and Mikell down as he was hauled away. None of the team members wanted anything to do with him after that point.

He was promptly booted from the team, and days later, word went around that he was expelled. One of the guys, who had an acquaintance that knew Asher better, actually said that he was so emotional in his questioning that he outed his cousin and some other accomplices, as well as implicated himself far worse than he really should have or needed to. He also went off on a racist rant, all witnessed by a black police captain. All of this was before he regained his composure and lawyered up. But the damage was long done, and Asher, as well as his extended family, would face the consequences.

***

The games that followed during the season were by no means easy to win. Mike and Mikell, as well as the other teammates, worked very hard on the court and endured one angry tirade from Lancing after another. Of course, he meant well, but his unique encouragement tactics took getting used to. The crowds their games drew became more diverse and more vocal as the games went on.

They traveled to other schools where they would secure wins, but none were blowouts, and they struggled and sweat for every single one. Several games came right down to the wire. In one instance they barely hung onto a tiny lead to end up with a win, and in the other Mikell sank a gorgeous jumper that had no business making it in at the buzzer, but a fortuitous bounce landed it through the net, as the team jumped with excitement.

They somehow managed to string together several victories in a row, enough to secure them a spot in the playoffs, though they did drop a game towards the season's end. That one was a particularly interesting event too. As they began to play, Mikell glanced at the opposing bench and saw a familiar face, it took him a few seconds to rummage his memory banks, but he realized that the face he was looking at reminded him a whole lot of the kid on the train.

Once the two connected eyes, the kid grew especially nervous. It turns out that two of the other kids were on the same team, but the fight on the train got them both suspended from the team from the various video accounts in the investigation. The kid who remained was on the outs with his coach and rode the bench most of the time, but stayed on as a technicality based on the fact that his participation was minimal compared to the others, at least in what the video accounts showed.

Mikell had hoped that the kid would be an on-the-court opponent and even talked about it to Mike at halftime. They both committed to a "hard-foul" but they never got the chance as the kid never entered the game. Afterward, they agreed it was probably for the best.

***

The team made the playoffs and blasted past the first-round opponents. Their winning record at the end of the season ranked them as a respectable 9th place among the 16 teams who qualified, so their first matchup was a team comparable to them in the record. The first game ended with a comfortable 10-point victory, but the next game would be a lot tougher.

Mike managed to foul out of the game, and the lead kept changing by two or three points for the entire fourth quarter until the closing seconds. James lobbed an assist to Mikell for a dunk, securing a two-point lead when the game was tied with 20 seconds to go. The opposing team then lost the ball carelessly out of bounds with 6 seconds on the clock, and the squad was able to hang on to the two-point lead for the rest of the game.

Lancing asked the team to consider how far they had come from the start of the season. He jokingly asked the team to give Mike a round of applause for fouling out so that he could make sure he didn't screw up the team's win, then praised the squad for their exceptional efforts against a very tough opponent. Then Lancing warned that their next matchup would be against the number 3 seated team, and the semi-finals, which everyone was shocked they actually made it to would be a very difficult one to overcome.

***

Mikell and Mike both practiced very hard during the following week and with the team's current trajectory, they were cautiously optimistic about the upcoming matchup. When the day came, the pressure was really on. And the pressure was not just on the court against a stellar team. Both of Mike's parents were at the game, as were Pops, and Lucia. She even brought her mom and her younger sister with her. Lucia had wanted Mike to meet her mother and the other way around. Perhaps if her mom saw Mike perform on the court, she would be more impressed. Though Lucia knew full well that her mom would not rank basketball talents among the top qualifiers as a good match for her daughter, she knew Mike's personality would win her over. He managed to be net-neutral on the topic of protecting her daughter (plus points) while getting into a fight that became very public (minus points) for her mom already.

The game was a hotly contested matchup, but Mike delivered big, especially in the third quarter, ranking up 4 timely three-pointers, all pushing the team's lead further and further ahead. In the closing minutes, the game was within 5 points, and Mike drove down the lane, through a sea of defenders. When he knew he had no chance, he went up into the air, but instead of attempting a sure-to-fail layup, Mike blasted the ball to the side into Mikell's hands. With all the defenders swarming Mike, they let their guard slip off everyone else, allowing Mikell to soar over them to nail a dunk.

The final minutes brought more pressure as the opponents nailed a three-pointer to bring the game to within four points, and the shooting player was fouled in the process. After he missed his free throw, Mikell rebounded and sent the ball up to a racing Mike down the court, who completed the breakaway layup, giving the team a six-point lead. With seconds to go, the opponents managed to get another basket, but their time ran out, and just like that the school advanced into the finals.

None of the playoff games were at home, simply because the team didn't rank high enough for that to be the case, but the celebration with many of the families and friends in the crowd was still intense.

Lucia hugged Mike on the court, introducing her mother and sister. Mike's parents were right there to celebrate. Mike's dad had a big proud smile for his son, a welcome change from his usual stone-faced demenour. He was very cordial in the introduction to Lucia and her family, and Mike's mother couldn't stop gushing about her pride in her son.

Mikell led Pops over to introduce him to Mike and his family. There was a moment of apprehension. Mike's dad had been the head of a project at Travis's last job, where a round of layoffs was partially made by Mike's father. Mike's father asked if Pops needed work, and while Pops, prideful as he was said he was fine, Mike's father said to let him know if there was a time he needed help. They even exchanged phone numbers.

Once everyone was heading home, Mike's mom informed him that she and his father were heading to see his brother. He called them the day before, sounding mournful and clean, and wanted to talk. She wasn't sure what this entailed, but it would hopefully be positive. Gradually everyone headed home, while Mike and Mikell decided to walk together and chat about the win, their lives, and the latest on the rap scene.

***

"Come on, we barely survived that one man, we are playing a number 1 seed in the finals. We are a damn Cinderella story. The talk of high school basketball in Boston, for less than shitty reasons this time too. You can't honestly think we are going to beat these guys do you?" - Mike said to Mikell as they started the shootaround at the final practice.

"You were probably thinking the same defeatist shit when we started the season with a losing record. Then when we were in the first round, the second, and the semis. Is that your thing? Lowering expectations so you don't get disappointed?" - Mikell said, sounding like some sort of psychoanalyst.

Mike stared at him. "I can get a shrink if I needed a consult, doc. I am just saying that we are outmatched, on every level. It don't mean I'm not gonna play hard, or that I'm admitting defeat. Just keepin' it real."

"You love to keep things real....real pessimistic. I don't know about you but the rest of the team and I are not looking at taking this as a minor victory. We are in the

262

finals, son. We need to see this through. Turnaround of this story would be incredible." - Mikell shot back.

Mike took a shot, sinking a jumper. "I'll celebrate with the rest of you if we pull this off, but I will sleep calmly if we don't, knowing we got this far considering the rest of the shit this season. I will admit, for some people who were getting their asses handed to them, we fought back pretty well. In more sense than one." - Mike said as he pulled up for another jumper which rattled around the rim.

"Little less brotherly banter, little more making shots boys!" - came Lancing's voice from behind them.

Mike and Mikell glanced at each other and parted to focus on their practice. Lancing walked around arms folded watching the team and making unsolicited comments to his players. One would think he would take it a little easy on the team seeing as they did the unthinkable and made it to the finals. But he was as much of a hardass as ever. Though it was probably for the best.

***

It was game day. The crowd piled in early, eager with anticipation. Mike, Mikell, and a few other guys from the team stepped outside to get some fresh air before coming out to the court. The crowd filing into the building was huge. It reminded Mike of the corner into

Paradise Rock Club the night of Sleepy's show. He felt and looked a lot better this time around.

Regardless of the result today, the team was damn proud of their accomplishments. The pressure came off everyone's relationships since Asher's poisonous presence was removed from the equation. The team was a lot more focused and undivided. The stellar accomplishments they achieved didn't hurt matters either.

A glass bottle hit the ground in the distance. Mike and Mikell whipped their heads around, undesirable memories of times they'd rather forget rattling in their minds. It looked like a kid dropped a glass Coke bottle that their parent asked them to go toss in the trash can. The thing didn't smash, just rattled around and rolled to a stop. The little boy ran after it, picked it up, and turned around to show his dad that it was fine, to which his father nodded approvingly.

The guys headed inside just in time for coming out to the gym for the pregame shootaround. Mike saw Lucia sitting with her friends towards the front. She waved to him with a big smile and he waved back. Lancing was busy plotting strategy with his fellow coaches, then headed over to greet the opposing team's coach.

Soon it was time for the national anthem to be played and the crowd stood ceremonially in silence, hands over their hearts. The team stood side by side eager with anticipation. The excitement of the moment permeated the gym and the electricity could be felt by everyone present. The teams took the court with Mike starting at shooting guard this time and Mikell at power forward. Everyone greeted the opposing starting five and took their positions on the court. The lead official came up to the center and looked around.

The crowd was on their feet, excited and cheering for the game to begin. The players set themselves as both teams' centers lined up opposite each other at center court. The ref looked around again, then stepped up to the center looked up in the air, and blew his whistle tossing the ball up between the two for opening tip-off. Game on!

Made in the USA
Middletown, DE
23 August 2022